GW00707585

MORE SHARES FOR YOUR MONEY

ROSTERS LTD.

MORE SHARES FOR YOUR MONEY

A guide to buying investment trust shares

Sponsored by the

Association of Investment Trust Companies

Published by ROSTERS LTD.
23 Welbeck Street, London W1M 7PG

© Rosters 1991
ISBN 1-85631-011-6

This book is sold subject to the condition that it shall not, by way
of trade or otherwise, be lent, re-sold, hired out or otherwise
circulated without the publisher's prior consent in any form of
binding or cover other than that in which it is published and without
a similar condition being imposed on the subsequent purchaser.

All rights reserved. No part of this book may be
reproduced or transmitted by any means without
prior permission.

First edition written by Christine Stopp
This edition by Rosemary Burr

Designed and published by ROSTERS
Typeset by Busbys (The Printers) Ltd , Exeter, Devon
Printed and bound in Great Britain by Cox & Wyman Ltd, Reading

Foreword by Michael Hart, Chairman of The Association of Investment Trust Companies

I welcome this new edition of More Shares For Your Money. Investment trusts are the most cost effective way for the private investor to get involved in equity investments. Investment Trust savings schemes which were introduced in 1984 have proved very popular and have been growing strongly in recent years. The problem of choosing particular shares and getting the timing right is solved by investment trust monthly savings schemes.

At one time investment trusts were considered a bit of a mystery but this is no longer the case. The attractions of investment trusts are increasingly being recognised. Financial journalists now devote much more space to covering and explaining the industry.

The concept of an investment trust company is a simple one. They are companies whose business is buying and selling and holding investments. However, there are many variations around the basic theme.

This book explains the industry in considerable depth but in a simple and straightforward way.

Since 1945 the average investment trust with income reinvested would have turned a £1,000 investment into £200,000. On the same basis a building society deposit would now be worth £8,000. All private investors should consider investment trusts for a proportion of their savings. "More shares for your money" explains how to go about it.

Contents

CHAPTER ONE:
PERFORMANCE COUNTS

Everyone likes to buy something at a discount, and with investment trusts discounts are a fact of life. That's why we've called this book *More shares for your money*. What *is* an investment trust, and why can it so often be had at a 'sale price'?

An investment trust is a company with shares quoted on the Stock Exchange, just like Marks & Spencer or British Telecom, or any other company whose name you might be familiar with and which you might even hold shares in. Unlike other companies, the investment trust's form of trading may seem rather passive. It doesn't operate factories, fleets of vehicles or have a sales force. Its purpose in life is to invest in other companies which may go in for any or all of these activities and by doing so to give the best possible return to its shareholders.

Perhaps you bought shares in British Telecom when they were launched in late 1984. You may have sold very quickly and made a considerable profit. Alternatively, you may have held on to the shares as a long term investment. If you still had your Telecom shares in mid-January 1991, you were probably feeling quite pleased with your gain. By the end of 1990 if you had held on to your shares you would have seen a gain of 101%.

It is not hard to find an investment trust which performed as well or better over the same period. Foreign and Colonial Investment Trust, launched in 1868, is no newcomer to the market, but it saw its share price rise by nearly 138% over the same period. The London stock market as a whole was up by 57% over the same period.

Stock market performance

Whether you actually own shares or not, you may be one of the millions of investors who have become interested in the stock market over the last decade.

In 1987 stock markets around the world crashed and many investors began to realise that the words "shares prices can go down as well as up" were all too accurate.

However, for long-term investors, over say three or five years, investing in shares has proved a better bet than leaving your cash on deposit. That statement holds good for those investors who had to brave the market storms of the late 1980's. If you had invested £1,000 in the average investment trust on December 2, 1985 it would be showing a 69% paper increase by the end of 1990, compared to a 55% return on a building society deposit over the same period. Over a ten year timespan the average investment trust would have increased by around 330% compared to a building society deposit of around 230%.

While the figures for the performance of the average investment trust reinforce the message about the long term value of investment trusts for savers they do hide market differences in performance within the family of investment trusts. The table shows you the return achieved by both the best and the worst performing investment trust in each sector over both a five and ten year timespan.

SECTOR	FIVE YEARS %		TEN YEARS %	
	BEST	WORST	BEST	WORST
International (general)	229.58	−3.77	1047.44	269.92
International (capital growth)	120.98	33.29	439.05	271.75
International (income growth)	107.96	49.34	558.57	271.32
UK (general)	163.67	−36.79	619.96	25.24
UK (capital growth)	103.35	34.59	507.04	306.27
UK (income growth)	127.57	64.67	785.24	402.08
North America	22.80	12.43	201.71	127.72
Far East (incl. Japan)	158.82	20.64	434.36	155.53
Japan	185.60	85.63	653.03	530.42

9

Europe	104.46	−10.00	560.94	20.92
Financial and Property	42.39	4.42	274.01	225.01
Commodity and Energy	14.89	n/a	n/a	n/a
UK (smaller companies)	107.98	−21.05	423.06	50.99
Venture Capital	276.36	−52.01	515.02	−48.75
Split Capital (growth)	147.02	−8.7	656.10	125.00
Split Capital (income)	198.43	45.39	738.41	169.35
UK (High income)	37.34	−	164.54	−

Notes: Lump sum performance using offer to offer prices with income reinvested.

Source: Micropal. Data to 31.12.1990

As you can see it is vital to pick both the right sector and the right trust. In the next chapter we examine more closely the individual sectors and the performance of the industry as a whole. It is also important to keep in mind the importance of performance in relation to the overall performance of the chosen market. So for instance if you were assessing the investment performance of a UK general sector trust you might compare it to the FT All Share Index, a broad benchmarket of the price movements of major UK listed shares. Over five years to end December, 1990 the FT All Share Index rose by just over 74% and over ten years to end December, 1990 by 271%. So the best performing UK general investment trust outperformed the index by more than 100% over both five and ten years.

Industry's characteristics

Apart from the performance figures, which are evidence of the skilful management available in the investment trust industry, there are a number of points worth stressing:

- It has been going since the nineteenth century, but new trusts are still being formed to take advantage of potential investment opportunities.
- It is very varied both in the size and scope of its participants. There is room for small specialist funds as well as the large generalists.
- An overseas flavour is apparent. Foreign & Colonial, the industry's oldest trust, was set up to enable the small

10

investor to buy overseas government stocks. This flavour still persists, with relatively few trusts confining themselves to investment in the UK.

● The income objective. An overriding aim in life for the early trusts was to provide investors with a high income. Capital growth has now taken on a much greater relative importance, but trusts still offer the potential of growing income.

● Another important area of specialisation for investment trusts has been investing in smaller companies, including unlisted ones – that is, companies not quoted on a stock market. Investment in this type of company is difficult and risky for the smaller investor, but much less so for a specialist trust.

Knowing the pros

● Built in growth.

An investment trust is a share or equity investment, which means it has the possibility of capital growth as well as an income from dividends. In good times, growth over the medium to long term will be much better than the return on an interest-paying investment. Of course, share prices can fall as well as rise. All but very small investors should consider putting at least some of their capital into an equity investment, otherwise they could be missing out on growth.

● Cheap and easy.

Investment trusts are cheap and easy to buy. They do not have high commission charges built into the price, like insurance bonds and unit trusts. A small amount of commission is payable to the stockbroker when you buy and sell. There is little formality nowadays in buying investment trusts. It can be done over the phone, through a bank, or through one of the new high street 'share shops'.

● Spread of risk.

If you buy shares in a single company, your capital is wholly dependent on that one company's fortunes. The share price might fall dramatically, and a lot of your capital could be

11

wiped out. If you invest in a large number of shares, the risk is spread, because where one company might be performing badly, another will be performing well. Holding shares in a range of companies may even out the ups and downs, and reduces the risks of share investment. This is precisely what an investment trust does. It operates a pool, or portfolio, of shares. A single share in an investment trust might give you an interest in the fortunes of hundreds of different companies.

● Small can be beautiful.

Investment trusts are not the preserve of the very large investor, even though the large institutions are the major shareholders in the sector. In the last few years, a number of trusts have brought out regular savings schemes, through which you can buy investment trust shares with savings of as little as £20 a month. For the lump sum investor, £3,000 is a realistic minimum.

● Income as well.

Both income investors and those who are going for capital growth may be interested in investment trust shares. As we have seen, income may be a major objective for some trusts. It is true that you would not expect as high a starting yield from investment trusts as you would from the building society, but many of them have a record of steadily rising dividends, which make them well worth looking at as income investments.

● Special offer.

A distinctive feature of investment trusts is the discount. If you valued an investment trust by taking the number of shares in issue and multiplying by the quoted share price, you would in most cases get a lower figure than if you valued the portfolio of shares held by the trust at their individual market prices. In other words, you are buying an interest in all those shares at less than their market value, and you will have a bonus in the amount of those extra assets working for you. It is a bit like getting an extra 20 per cent free in a bottle of shampoo.

● In gear.

Another feature of investment trusts is *gearing*, which is a means of boosting the amount of assets from which you can achieve capital growth. An investment trust is allowed to borrow money which is used to buy more investments. The extent to which it makes use of this power is known as gearing. If the assets bought with the borrowed money increase in value, there will be a surplus left after the loan is repaid. That surplus becomes part of the shareholders' funds and thus adds to the growth of the *net asset value* of their ordinary shares. The revenue earned on those surplus assets in excess of the interest payable also generates more income for the shareholders.

● Spoiled for choice.

Whether your interest is in a UK investment or an overseas one, investment trusts offer plenty of choice. Some trusts invest in very specialised areas, like technology or smaller companies, though most have a broader approach, with shareholdings in a number of different markets and various different types of company. Investment trusts can invest in many things apart from shares, gilts and convertibles. They can, for instance, put money directly into properties or commodities, and they can, if necessary, get involved in the day-to-day running of businesses they have an interest in, rather than just acting as passive shareholders. As trusts differ so much in character, depending on their objectives, they can serve a number of different uses within an investor's own portfolio, from offering a low-yield, relatively high risk investment in a specialised market to providing a lower risk, broadly spread investment which offers income as well as capital growth.

● Low cost management

The portfolio of investments held by an investment trust is chosen and looked after by an investment manager. The management charge is shown in the trust's report and accounts, and will typically be around 0.4% or less as a percentage of total assets. Some trusts make higher charges if the markets they are investing in are specialised, hard to research, or

13

particularly demanding in management time. Even so their charges are considerably less than other packaged share products such as unit trusts, where annual charges of around 1½% are common.

● Long-term view.

The fact that the share capital of an investment trust is fixed is an advantage to the investment manager, because it means that he or she can take a long-term view of investment policy. With a fund which is sold in units rather than shares – for instance, a unit trust or a unit-linked insurance plan – the number of units in issue can go up or down. If new units are to be created or liquidated the manager may find he or she is expected to sell shares when the market is down, or buy when the market is high. The investment trust manager does not have this problem, and therefore can afford to make strategic investments, for instance in the venture capital market, where it may be some years before any major benefit is seen.

● Tax efficient.

An investment trust is also attractive to the investor from the point of view of tax. First of all, the trust itself pays no capital gains tax if it makes a profit on asset sales. This gives managers the flexibility to realise gains when market conditions prompt them to do so, instead of feeling inhibited by a large potential capital gains tax liability. Where the investor is concerned, there is no special exemption from tax on his own investment trust shareholdings, but his investment transactions can be planned so as to keep his liability to tax low or remove it altogether.

And the cons . . .?

There are many advantages to investment trusts, and relatively few disadvantages, some of which can be minimised by adopting a sensible and prudent approach and by making well informed investment decisions.

● **Ups and downs.**

Falling markets are the biggest risk with any form of equity investment, just as rising markets are the biggest advantage. If you put money into an investment trust which is itself invested in a sharply falling market, the best investment managers in the world will not be able to make you a profit. If you had invested all your capital in such a trust, you might feel that investment trusts were a disastrous investment. However, if you hold broadly spread investment trusts which are not dependent on one market's fortunes, this is unlikely to happen. Due to the inevitable ups and downs of any market, investment trust shareholders must be prepared for the spills – if only temporary – as well as the thrills. One broker tells each client that with any holding, there is likely to be a moment when he or she is showing a loss. If that thought brings you out in a cold sweat, then perhaps you should think twice about shares in any company.

● **Take your pick.**

With about 245 investment trusts on offer, it is hard to know which to choose. No one can predict which investment trust is going to perform best over the next few years, but this book aims to give you a start in choosing trusts with a steady performance record which will be suitable to your needs.

● **Think long term.**

It is quick and easy to get your money back when you sell investment trust shares. However, you should think of an investment trust as a long-term investment, because of what has already been said about rising and falling markets. 'Long-term' means two or three years at least in most cases. An investment trust is therefore not the place for money which you know you will need in six months' time.

● **Sounds unfamiliar.**

For investors used to building societies and insurance plans, an investment trust may seem unfamiliar. It is worth remembering that investment trusts are, in effect, simply managed portfolios of investments, most of which are traded

15

on the stockmarket and which have great freedom and flexibility to invest in securities and physical assets. Their performance record alone means they should not be ignored.

Who should invest?

There are many different categories of investor who can benefit from buying shares in investment trusts.

● Anyone looking for long-term growth, maybe in order to build up a nestegg for retirement, or just to earn a good return on money which will not be needed for a few years. As we have already seen, the growth record is the most attractive feature of this type of investment and many people are realising that it doesn't make sense to leave thousands of pounds in a building society account for several years when its value will be eroded by inflation.

● Those with a fairly small amount of money who want to venture into share investment, but feel they could not gain a wide enough spread by buying shares direct, or want to leave the choice of shares to someone else. For these investors, investment trust savings schemes are ideal.

● Long-term income seekers. As we have seen, an investment trust will not offer an income to rival the building society on day one, but over the years the income return should grow, eventually leaving the building society account behind.

● Investors who already have a share portfolio and want some exposure to overseas markets. For an individual it is hard to invest in foreign companies direct from the UK because to deal effectively, it will be necessary to assemble a 'package' of regular research information, dealing and price monitoring, safe custody of share certificates, and dividend collection. This can be time-consuming, expensive and probably uneconomical for all but the wealthiest private investor. An investment trust manager has much better market contacts than a lone investor and the management group may have offices in the countries where the relevant markets are situated. With foreign markets, currencies are a

16

major concern, and here again the trust is much better able to take decisions, and to hedge against currency risks, than the individual investor.

● Specialist investors. Specialist investment trusts have a rather higher risk element than general trusts, so may be suitable to the larger investor who wants specific exposure to one market or sector. Of particular interest are those trusts which have holdings in unquoted companies in the various world markets. Here, it is specially difficult for the private individual to choose companies and follow them, so professional management is even more important. For individual investors in unquoted companies, the biggest problem about such shares may be the difficulty of selling them should they want their money back. This problem will not arise if they hold the shares through an investment trust.

● People in or nearing retirement who want to build up savings and income, and who want an income which will go some way to keeping pace with inflation. Due to their ability to generate a growing income, investment trusts are suitable for this sort of investor. The record on income growth is very good.

● Younger working people, especially if they have a higher rate tax liability. They can choose low-yielding trusts to minimise their tax bill, while enjoying capital growth which, if they time their sales to avoid exceeding the capital gains tax exempt limit, is tax free.

● Younger investors. Investment trust shares, through a lump sum or a regular savings plan, make excellent gifts to children, who can leave the money invested in order to provide a cash sum when they are eighteen.

CHAPTER TWO:
THE INDUSTRY IN PROFILE

Two hundred investment trusts are members of The Association of Investment Trust Companies (AITC). Of these, approximately 130 are quoted daily among the 200 listed in the *Financial Times* and for the private investor these are the easiest to follow as the AITC publishes figures on them monthly. Different stock-brokers follow different lists of trusts, and some may include offshore funds, which are structured in the same way as a UK trust, and which may be quoted on the Stock Exchange.

The AITC places trusts into one of twenty categories:

Category	Definition	Number
International: general	Less than 80% assets in any one area.	20
International: capital growth	Less than 80% assets in any one area and aim to accentuate capital growth.	21
International: income growth	Less than 80% assets in any one area and aim to accentuate income growth.	4
UK: general	At least 80% assets in UK registered companies.	9
UK: capital growth	At least 80% assets in UK registered companies and aim to accentuate capital growth.	4
UK: income growth	At least 80% assets in UK registered companies and aim to accentuate income growth.	9
High income	At least 80% of assets in equities and aim for a yield in excess of 110% of FT All Shares Index.	

North America	At least 80% of assets in North America.	6
Far East (incl. Japan)	At least 80% of assets in Far East which includes a Japanese content of less than 80%.	8
Far East (excl. Japan)	At least 80% of assets in Far East, excluding any Japanese content.	14
Japan	At least 80% of assets in Japan.	5
Australasia	At least 80% of assets in Australasia	1
Europe	At least 80% of assets in Continental Europe	19
Financial and Property	At least 80% of assets in finance and property	2
Commodity and Energy	At least 80% of assets in commodities and energy	2
Technology	At least 80% of assets in technology	2
Smaller Companies	Majority of investments in companies with lower than average market capitalisation in each geographic area.	20
Venture Capital	Same rule as smaller companies but also 'positive policy' towards new ventures.	19
Split Capital Trusts	Trusts with income and capital shares which have fixed winding up dates.	16

Source: AITC (January 1990)

At the end of December 1990, the investment trust sector as monitored by stockbrokers County Nat West Wood Mac had a total market capitalisation of £14.77bn. The investment trust sector is equivalent in size to around 3.6% of the All-Share Index.

Individual trusts vary enormously in size. The five largest at 31 December 1990 were Foreign and Colonial, with a market capitalisation of £712m; Edinburgh Investment (£575m); Alliance (£526m); Witan (£449m) and Scottish Mortgage (£438m). County Nat West Wood Mac list forty other trusts with capitalisations of over £100m. At the other end of the scale, there were ninety trusts with capitalisations of less than £20m.

Specialisation develops

Investment trusts launched in the 1980s tended to have specialist investment objectives. Often they confined themselves to a single geographical area, such as Europe or the Far East, or even a single country. Such trusts had little or no yield. Their objective was not income, but capital growth, which was the main interest of investors in times when inflation had been seen to decimate asset values, when high income tax rates reduced the value of a dividend return, and when we were facing two decades or more of non-income producing retirement. Trusts are nowadays divided into groups partly on the strength of the relative importance they give to income or growth but chiefly by geographic content of the portfolio.

The tendency towards specialisation took place for a number of reasons. One was the movement towards increasing inter-nationalisation of world equity markets, making it easier to deal in shares round the world. Another was the 'cult of the equity' in the eighties, as more and more countries developed stock markets and encouraged investment in shares. Finally, it was a question of offering what the customer wanted: the institutions who were the main buyers of investment trust shares were often interested in narrowly specialised portofolios which they did not have the expertise to manage themselves.

The industry's long history has resulted in many trust names which give little indication of what the trust actually invests in, due to changes in investment objectives over the years. The investment trust industry has always had a leaning towards quaint or colourful names, and this is not merely due to history: 'Investing in Success', Mid Wynd and Marine Adventure Sailing are all relatively new trusts.

Of the more specialised sectors, North America is the least 'new-fangled'. America was regarded as the exciting new risk area for investment in the second half of the nineteenth century, and several of the trusts in this small category are among the oldest in the industry. There are a number of trusts which still retain some reference to North America in their title, but which have long since switched to other investment objectives. If

America was 'flavour of the century' a hundred years ago, Japan and the Far East occupied the equivalent position in the eighties. The amazing growth record of the Japanese economy has been built up since World War II, and most of the Japan investment trusts have been launched since 1970, though some more general Far Eastern trusts are much older.

In the more sober nineties as investment trusts are increasingly marketed to consumers it appears likely that more general run-of-the-mill UK and international trusts will increase in popularity. The moves towards relaxing the restrictions on cold-calling when marketing investment trusts and towards greater flexibility in using investment trusts in pension plans means that this trend should accelerate throughout the early nineties.

New categories

Other specialists categories reflect prevailing investment fashions. New categories such as Europe, Australasia, commodity/energy and technology are recent developments in more specialised areas or smaller markets. Trusts in some of these categories take advantage of the investment trust's freedom to invest in unquoted exploration or research stocks, and to own dealing subsidiaries whose sole business might be, for example, in commodity futures.

The smaller companies category reflects another traditional specialisation of investment trusts. Companies in the early stages of corporate development tend to have a sharper growth curve than mature companies, though there is a higher risk of failure. Smaller companies trust portfolios often include a percentage of unquoteds.

The category which really specialises in unquoted companies, however, is venture capital. This includes the trusts which have the highest percentage of unquoted investments in the sector, and which cover the widest range of unquoteds.

Among the venture capital trusts are those which provide finance at the early stages of a company's development, known as 'venture capital' and 'development capital' and those which help to finance management buy-outs. This sector may also include companies which appear to have strong growth prospects for any number of special reasons. They may be takeover targets, for instance, or companies undergoing a change of management.

Doing the splits

The final AITC category is the split level trusts. These trusts are categorised according to their structure, rather than their investment objective, which tends to be general with a high UK bias. They provide two classes of shares, one for investors who want income and one for those who want growth.

Most trusts, as the venerable old giants indicate, just go on and on. Split level trusts, though, have a fixed winding-up date. These are known as 'limited life trusts'. When shares are first issued, a date will be fixed on or by which investors have to vote on whether the trust should be wound up or not. When a trust is wound up its investments are sold, the creditors are paid off and the balance shared out among the shareholders. The trust then ceases to trade.

The money managers

Finally, who are the companies which manage investment trusts? Many have a very long history in the City and the business of investment management. Some actually date back to the last century, like Ivory & Sime, established in 1895, or even older trust managers originating from the merchant banking sector, like Hambros Bank (1839) or Morgan Grenfell (1838).

Other groups are modern reincarnations of older entities, like Robert Fleming, a modern management group with one of the oldest names in the sector, or F & C, which manages the oldest trust. Then there are groups set up during the early decades of this century, like Baillie Gifford (1908), a small partnership which manages several hundred million pounds, or Henderson (1934), which started out as the manager to the Henderson family trust and developed into a household name. Most investment trust managers are also well known names in the unit trust and pension industry as well.

The sixties, seventies and eighties saw no shortage of new management groups, often formed by one or two high-flying individuals who gained their experience in older companies and then decided to 'go it alone'. GT (1969) is a well-known example of this, where the original partnership has since divided again, leading to the formation of a new management group, Thornton Management (1985).

An investment trust management group may be a wholly owned subsidiary of the trust or trusts which it manages. There has been a tendency in the past few years for management groups to be set up as separate entities permitted to take on new business, such as unit trust and pensions management. The aim is to make the management subsidiary a profit-making company rather than a passive service organisation.

Investment Trust Categories

31 December 1990

Total assets £ million	High/ low pence	Share price pence	NAV pence	Discount (-Premium) %	Gearing	UK	N.America	Japan	Far East	Cont. Europe	Other
								Geographical spread			
624	1234/960	1044	1230	15	96	51	30	3	4	12	-
169	100/75	80	95	17	102	56	22	2	3	17	-
486	665/530	540	655	18	109	67	10	4	7	12	-
116	177/128	137	155	12	106	69	13	2	6	10	-
-	585/225	275	-	-	-	-	-	-	-	-	-
5	50/28	32	38	17	100	45	15	11	10	18	1
771	236/180	197	224	12	99	69	9	6	4	12	-
982	174/125	136	151	11	113	47	25	10	3	14	1
34	328/241	241	295	18	103	56	12	4	4	20	4
149	165/123	133	158	16	104	74	12	3	2	9	-
-	400/318	336	-	-	-	-	-	-	-	-	-
14	273/218	218	232	6	88	25	17	5	12	40	1
8	53/35	35	50	31	82	69	31	-	-	-	-
304	119/89	96	113	15	105	61	12	4	5	18	-
417	64/47	49	57	15	110	57	16	9	2	13	3
495	177/132	141	165	15	98	46	19	8	6	21	-
620	151/113	122	142	14	114	59	14	5	4	16	2
211	1080/860	922	1090	15	97	50	30	3	4	13	-
134	247/188	202	235	14	95	61	14	7	4	14	-
599	164/123	132	153	14	98	68	16	5	2	9	-
341				15	101	57	18	5	5	15	1

* This trust is currently (and it is understood, temporarily) outside the criteria accorded to its category.
† SS = Savings Scheme

· INTERNATIONAL: GENERAL ·

Investment trusts with less than 80% of their assets in any one geographical area.

Trust	Share price total return			NAV total return			5yr Div growth %	Gross yield %	SS†
	1yr	5yrs	10yrs	1yr	5yrs	10yrs			
ALLIANCE	86.6	173.5	568.2	87.4	160.4	474.4	+102.9	4.9	✓
BANKERS	84.4	182.3	610.7	85.2	168.3	522.1	+113.8	4.7	✓
BRITISH INVESTMENT	85.5	174.5	480.9	82.3	154.8	397.1	+51.4	5.4	✓
BRUNNER	81.5	192.9	522.1	77.6	160.7	415.4	+95.5	4.2	✓
CAPITAL GEARING	50.5	314.4	1085.8	-	-	-	+62.5	0.2	
CASTLE CAIRN	-	-	-	-	-	-	-	-	
EDINBURGH INVESTMENT	88.4	192.8	451.2	83.0	156.8	420.2	+145.6	4.9	✓
FOREIGN & COLONIAL	82.2	211.3	560.2	77.3	169.0	448.1	+94.6	2.8	✓
GREENFRIAR	77.9	119.1	437.1	74.6	131.2	430.7	+200.8	2.2	✓
KLEINWORT CHARTER	84.7	176.5	516.3	82.0	162.2	421.9	+106.9	4.8	✓
LAW DEBENTURE	90.8	206.3	644.9	-	-	-	+145.5	5.7	
MID WYND INTERNATIONAL	88.2	147.9	-	78.8	135.4	-	+114.0	2.8	✓
PERSONAL ASSETS	69.1	96.4	-	77.9	123.6	-	+400.0	5.8	✓
SCOTTISH AMERICAN	85.3	158.3	391.3	84.3	147.9	344.9	+135.7	5.3	✓
SCOTTISH EASTERN	79.6	175.8	482.3	78.5	153.6	402.8	+85.6	3.3	✓
SCOTTISH INVESTMENT	83.5	160.6	462.3	79.8	142.9	354.3	+103.5	3.8	✓
SCOTTISH MORTGAGE	84.8	167.3	540.5	82.1	143.7	448.2	+123.3	3.8	✓
SECOND ALLIANCE	91.0	186.1	606.8	86.9	162.0	482.0	+103.1	4.8	✓
TRIBUNE	85.0	197.7	561.4	81.7	166.8	457.2	+131.1	4.0	✓
WITAN	85.8	173.2	530.1	81.1	156.5	437.5	+227.3	4.5	✓
AVERAGE	82.4	179.3	556.0	81.2	152.7	430.5	+133.8	4.1	

· INTERNATIONAL: CAPITAL GROWTH ·

General investment trusts with less than 80% of their assets in any

Total assets £ million	High/ low pence	Share price pence	NAV pence	Discount (-Premium) %	Gearing	Geographical spread					
						UK	N.America	Japan	Far East	Cont.Europe	Other
342	317/207	221	267	17	109	45	22	19	4	10	-
17	100/58	58	74	22	90	2	4	·	25	38	31
179	569/382	394	468	16	93	23	20	23	7	27	-
14	50/38	42	48	14	25	100	-	-	-	-	-
108	123/88	91	112	19	92	59	23	3	3	11	1
127	145/106	110	131	16	82	57	17	5	3	17	1
249	247/147	156	187	17	99	7	37	22	10	24	-
2	305/225	245	281	13	71	92	-	-	-	4	4
127	185/125	131	157	17	93	19	29	19	7	25	1
-	46/32	32	-	-	-	-	-	-	-	-	-
-	96/62	73	-	-	-	-	-	-	-	-	-
294	359/272	287	327	12	96	50	18	2	9	19	2
134	273/185	198	223	11	102	23	9	3	39	25	1
86	75/52	52	63	18	94	18	26	-	30	2	24
87	283/172	189	227	17	103	-	33	34	8	25	-
7	188/111	111	153	28	89	67	17	-	7	9	-
-	120/80	90	-	-	-	-	-	-	-	-	-
53	131/77	77	107	28	161	56	23	7	9	3	2
20	150/124	124	154	20	102	50	16	8	2	23	1
62	182/141	145	169	15	75	44	17	5	12	19	3
-	435/395	395	-	-	-	-	-	-	-	-	-
112				18	93	42	18	9	10	17	4

· INTERNATIONAL: INCOME GROWTH ·

General investment trusts with less than 80% of their assets in any

Total assets £ million	High/ low pence	Share price pence	NAV pence	Discount (-Premium) %	Gearing	Geographical spread					
						UK	N.America	Japan	Far East	Cont.Europe	Other
486	83/64	67	80	17	148	78	19	-	2	1	-
12	101/68	75	82	9	77	76	10	3	5	4	2
343	252/195	196	220	11	96	52	21	3	11	13	-
225	72/55	61	63	4	103	70	18	4	2	6	-
267				10	106	69	17	3	5	6	1

26

· INTERNATIONAL: CAPITAL GROWTH ·

one geographical area, whose policy is to accentuate capital growth.

Trust	Share price total return			NAV total return			5yr Div growth %	Gross yield %	SS
	1yr	5yrs	10yrs	1yr	5yrs	10yrs			
ANGLO & OVERSEAS	72.2	166.9	461.2	73.4	149.8	388.4	+96.5	3.5	✓
BETA GLOBAL EMERGING	-	-	-	-	-	-	-	-	
DUNEDIN WORLDWIDE	71.7	153.8	421.4	72.1	134.2	349.6	+66.7	3.0	✓
ECU TRUST	-	-	-	-	-	-	-	-	
ELECTRIC & GENERAL	79.5	174.6	517.9	80.5	157.1	432.7	+316.7	4.4	✓
ENGLISH & SCOTTISH	79.1	158.1	412.3	77.6	146.7	370.0	+120.0	3.8	✓
FLEMING OVERSEAS	67.3	137.4	388.3	69.8	126.0	320.3	+45.5	3.4	✓
HOTSPUR INVESTMENTS*	-	-	-	-	-	-	+284.6	3.0	
KLEINWORT OVERSEAS	72.9	127.3	393.9	74.3	123.1	320.9	+20.0	3.5	✓
LATIN AMERICAN SECURITIES	-	-	-	-	-	-	-	-	✓
MERLIN INTERNATIONAL GREEN	74.0	-	-	-	-	-	-	4.1	
MONKS	84.5	191.0	519.7	82.3	163.1	428.1	+150.0	2.9	✓
MURRAY SMALLER MARKETS	74.4	195.1	631.8	78.0	175.1	508.1	+164.0	2.3	✓
NEW FRONTIERS DEV	71.9	-	-	72.0	-	-	-	0.6	✓
OVERSEAS	68.3	138.7	385.8	72.6	137.6	318.2	+41.2	1.7	✓
PRIMADONNA	64.2	-	-	72.7	-	-	-	4.8	
RIT CAPITAL PARTNERS	79.7	-	-	-	-	-	-	3.9	
SELECTIVE ASSETS	61.5	-	-	72.3	-	-	-	1.1	✓
STRATTON	86.5	-	-	84.0	-	-	-	1.2	
USDC	82.7	-	-	81.3	-	-	-	3.6	✓
UPDOWN	97.0	197.6	580.4	-	-	-	+143.2	30	
AVERAGE	75.7	164.1	471.3	75.9	145.9	381.8	+131.7	3.0	

· INTERNATIONAL: INCOME GROWTH ·

one geographical area, whose policy is to accentuate income growth.

Trust	Share price total return			NAV total return			5yr Div growth %	Gross yield %	SS
	1yr	5yrs	10yrs	1yr	5yrs	10yrs			
BRITISH ASSETS	86.8	145.8	419.1	86.7	132.8	382.7	+116.9	7.7	✓
JERSEY PHOENIX	78.7	-	-	86.7	-	-	-	7.5	
MURRAY INTERNATIONAL	83.5	164.0	552.8	79.9	144.1	407.6	+126.7	6.9	✓
SECURITIES TRUST OF SCOTLAND	92.4	212.5	689.9	85.1	170.8	502.7	+182.0	6.5	✓
AVERAGE	85.4	174.1	553.9	84.6	149.2	431.0	+141.9	7.2	

· UK: GENERAL ·

Investment trusts with at least 80% of

Total assets £ million	High/low pence	Share price pence	NAV pence	Discount (-Premium) %	Gearing	Geographical spread					
						UK	N.America	Japan	Far East	Cont.Europe	Other
17	97/68	68	87	22	-	100	-	-	-	-	-
74	306/235	274	293	6	120	100	-	-	-	-	-
293	276/160	162	200	19	83	85	8	2	-	5	-
14	160/129	129	152	15	90	77	2	5	1	14	1
65	424/346	351	397	12	103	79	8	3	-	10	-
46	99/84	90	95	5	98	100	-	-	-	-	-
22	122/93	93	91	-2	101	97	1	-	-	-	2
26	735/625	655	769	15	109	99	1	-	-	-	-
171	270/205	222	264	16	91	100	-	-	-	-	-
81				12	99	93	2	1	0	3	0

· UK: CAPITAL GROWTH ·

UK specialists with at least 80% of their assets in UK-registered

Total assets £ million	High/low pence	Share price pence	NAV pence	Discount (-Premium) %	Gearing	Geographical spread					
						UK	N.America	Japan	Far East	Cont.Europe	Other
8	176/112	112	148	24	90	86	-	-	12	-	2
-	56/45	45	-	-	-	-	-	-	-	-	-
75	149/122	134	160	16	104	100	-	-	-	-	-
-	46/35	35	-	-	-	-	-	-	-	-	-
2	83/68	72	-	-	-	80	18	-	-	2	-
42				20	97	88	6	0	4	1	1

· UK: INCOME GROWTH ·

UK specialists with at least 80% of their assets in UK-registered

Total assets £ million	High/low pence	Share price pence	NAV pence	Discount (-Premium) %	Gearing	Geographical spread					
						UK	N.America	Japan	Far East	Cont.Europe	Other
196	518/405	452	489	8	107	95	-	-	-	5	-
22	101/80	85	84	0	97	97	-	-	-	-	3
42	102/77	77	76	-1	184	100	-	-	-	-	-
255	107/84	96	100	4	98	100	-	-	-	-	-
47	201/154	160	173	7	106	91	1	-	2	6	-
227	202/155	174	191	9	108	95	5	-	-	-	

† Savings Scheme run by Argosy

28

· UK: GENERAL ·

their assets in UK-registered companies.

Trust	Share price total return			NAV total return			5yr Div growth %	Gross yield %	SS
	1yr	5yrs	10yrs	1yr	5yrs	10yrs			
ANGLO SCANDINAVIAN	74.1	-	-	-	-	-	-	8.9	
FLEMING CLAVERHOUSE	96.9	212.1	644.9	85.0	174.1	493.7	+95.4	4.6	✓
GOVETT STRATEGIC	64.1	97.2	258.9	62.9	89.1	225.1	+108.3	6.2	✓
JOS HOLDINGS*	85.3	166.7	500.7	81.4	166.3	473.3	+113.4	5.2	✓
KEYSTONE*	86.8	194.0	581.2	84.6	164.4	473.2	+160.0	3.8	✓
MALVERN UK	-	-	-	-	-	-	-	5.4	✓
SCOTTISH & MERCANTILE	79.7	144.0	384.5	79.2	120.7	240.3	+24.3	5.0	
SCOTTISH CITIES	102.2	179.8	423.8	86.0	164.3	306.0	+17.4	5.5	
TEMPLE BAR	88.2	191.9	598.8	86.9	182.7	537.3	+119.4	6.4	✓
AVERAGE	84.7	169.4	484.7	80.9	151.7	392.7	+91.2	5.7	

· UK: CAPITAL GROWTH ·

companies, whose policy is to accentuate capital growth.

Trust	Share price total return			NAV total return			5yr Div growth %	Gross yield %	SS
	1yr	5yrs	10yrs	1yr	5yrs	10yrs			
BERRY STARQUEST	65.9	-	-	69.0	-	-	-	1.8	✓
BRITISH EMPIRE SECURITIES	80.8	148.0	-	-	-	-	+56.0	2.3	✓†
FLEMING ENTERPRISE	97.4	202.7	648.0	94.2	201.4	568.8	+78.8	3.8	✓
MULTITRUST	85.4	-	-	-	-	-	-	3.8	
NEW GUERNSEY SECURITIES	96.0	-	-	78.0	-	-	-	-	
AVERAGE	85.1	175.4	648.0	80.4	201.4	568.8	+67.4	2.9	

· UK: INCOME GROWTH ·

companies, whose policy is to accentuate income growth.

Trust	Share price total return			NAV total return			5yr Div growth %	Gross yield %	SS
	1yr	5yrs	10yrs	1yr	5yrs	10yrs			
DUNEDIN INCOME GROWTH	95.8	184.1	602.4	85.2	159.7	447.0	+211.1	6.5	✓
HENDERSON HIGHLAND	-	-	-	-	-	-	-	8.3	✓
I & S OPTIMUM INCOME	83.1	-	-	75.9	-	-	-	11.9	✓
INVESTORS CAPITAL	98.6	188.0	-	88.5	166.4	-	+317.0	6.8	✓
LOWLAND	85.4	161.2	893.1	82.0	177.5	765.0	+176.8	6.5	✓
MERCHANTS	92.9	200.7	548.3	85.8	173.5	421.1	+166.7	6.9	✓

· UK: INCOME GROWTH ·

UK specialists with at least 80% of their assets in UK-registered

Total assets £ million	High/low pence	Share price pence	NAV pence	Discount (-Premium) %	Gearing	Geographical spread					
						UK	N.America	Japan	Far East	Cont.Europe	Other
197	239/196	211	235	10	95	81	9	-	1	9	-
210	106/85	96	100	3	103	100	-	-	-	-	-
45	61/56	56	72	23	130	100	-	-	-	-	-
138				7	114	95	2	0	0	2	0

· HIGH INCOME ·

Trusts which invest at least 80% of their assets in equities and which aim

Total assets £ million	High/low pence	Share price pence	NAV pence	Discount (-Premium) %	Gearing	Geographical spread					
						UK	N.America	Japan	Far East	Cont.Europe	Other
17	52/34	37	33	-12	282	100	-	-	-	-	-
36	100/88	94	92	-1	-	100	-	-	-	-	-
20	100/85	90	81	-11	80	95	-	-	-	-	5
72	46/24	24	25	3	242	30	23	-	7	26	14
52	48/27	28	24	-16	445	98	1	-	1	-	-
12	51/37	39	40	4	-	100	-	-	-	-	-
-	102/42	46	-	-	-	-	-	-	-	-	-
25	95/57	65	51	-26	278	100	-	-	-	-	-
46	108/89	91	84	-7	156	99	-	-	-	-	1
74	237/187	201	213	6	-	96	3	-	-	-	1
89	44/24	24	21	-15	287	39	19	3	7	30	2
12	108/86	86	86	0	78	100	-	-	-	-	-
41				-7	231	87	4	0	1	5	2

· NORTH AMERICA ·

Investment trusts with at least 80% of

Total assets £ million	High/low pence	Share price pence	NAV pence	Discount (-Premium) %	Gearing	Geographical spread					
						UK	N.America	Japan	Far East	Cont.Europe	Other
135	181/120	131	159	18	91	23	77	-	-	-	-
132	184/118	134	158	16	95	2	98	-	-	-	-
35	43/23	23	28	20	270	23	77	-	-	-	-
79	101/65	65	90	28	166	-	100	-	-	-	-
131	183/119	132	160	18	95	9	91	-	-	-	-
7	83/38	38	55	31	88	1	99	-	-	-	-
87				22	134	10	90	0	0	0	0

· UK: INCOME GROWTH ·

companies, whose policy is to accentuate income growth.

Trust	Share price total return			NAV total return			5yr Div growth %	Gross yield %	SS
	1yr	5yrs	10yrs	1yr	5yrs	10yrs			
MURRAY INCOME	95.0	192.6	704.2	89.6	178.2	550.2	+80.0	6.3	✓
TR CITY OF LONDON	99.0	232.1	777.8	91.1	197.7	572.2	+138.6	6.3	✓
VALUE & INCOME	98.3	-	-	100.9	-	-	+450.0	6.5	
AVERAGE	93.5	193.1	705.2	87.4	175.5	551.1	+220.0	7.3	

· HIGH INCOME ·

to achieve a yield in excess of 110% of the FT Actuaries All Share Index.

Trust	Share price total return			NAV total return			5yr Div growth %	Gross yield %	SS
	1yr	5yrs	10yrs	1yr	5yrs	10yrs			
CITY OF OXFORD - ORD	81.1	-	-	65.7	-	-	-	16.4	✓
DARTMOOR	-	-	-	-	-	-	-	14.3	
FLEMING HIGH INCOME	97.4	-	-	87.6	-	-	-	8.6	✓
FLEMING INT HIGH INCOME - ORD	59.6	-	-	53.8	-	-	-	15.0	✓
GARTMORE VALUE - ORD	72.1	-	-	53.3	-	-	-	19.3	✓
GLASGOW INCOME	83.1	-	-	82.0	-	-	-	10.9	✓
LONDON & NEW YORK	47.7	-	-	-	-	-	-	18.7	
OLIM CONVERTIBLE - ORD	78.2	-	-	64.5	-	-	-	16.8	
RIVER & MERC EXTRA INCOME	94.2	-	-	90.6	-	-	-	11.4	
SHIRES	94.4	141.8	273.5	87.3	140.2	283.5	+34.0	11.5	✓
SPHERE	59.5	-	-	49.0	-	-	-	22.0	
TR HIGH INCOME	82.5	-	-	89.4	-	-	-	9.3	✓
AVERAGE	77.3	141.8	273.5	72.3	140.2	283.5	+34.0	14.5	

· NORTH AMERICA ·

their assets in North America.

Trust	Share price total return			NAV total return			5yr Div growth %	Gross yield %	SS
	1yr	5yrs	10yrs	1yr	5yrs	10yrs			
AMERICAN*	76.1	110.3	272.9	82.4	111.1	240.5	+55.2	4.6	✓
FLEMING AMERICAN	74.5	112.1	316.4	78.7	108.8	259.8	+13.6	1.5	✓
GARTMORE AMERICAN* - ORD	60.3	-	-	63.0	-	-	+70.0	20.1	✓
GOVETT AMERICAN	-	-	-	-	-	-	-	16.0	
GOVETT ATLANTIC	74.4	114.4	238.6	78.8	107.5	204.6	+25.0	3.5	✓
LEVERAGED OPPORTUNITY TRUST	46.9	-	-	-	-	-	-	-	
AVERAGE	66.4	112.3	276.0	75.7	109.1	235.0	+41.0	9.1	

31

· FAR EAST: INCLUDING JAPAN ·
Investment trusts with at least 80% of their assets in Far Eastern

Total assets £ million	High/ low pence	Share price pence	NAV pence	Discount (-Premium) %	Gearing	Geographical spread					
						UK	N.America	Japan	Far East	Cont.Europe	Other
96	146/76	83	84	2	86	8	-	30	59	-	3
185	221/134	135	167	19	88	1	23	40	35	-	1
315	298/148	161	199	17	97	1	-	39	60	-	-
310	516/264	277	314	12	112	-	-	31	67	-	2
28	298/189	205	221	7	90	3	-	57	40	-	-
34	106/60	61	73	16	95	9	-	-	91	-	-
62	104/54	66	62	-7	90	1	-	6	90	-	3
147				9	94	3	3	29	63	0	1

· FAR EAST: EXCLUDING JAPAN ·
Investment trusts with at least 80% of their assets in Far

Total assets £ million	High/ low pence	Share price pence	NAV pence	Discount (-Premium) %	Gearing	Geographical spread					
						UK	N.America	Japan	Far East	Cont.Europe	Other
27	143/68	73	89	18	85	2	-	-	85	-	13
9	101/45	48	60	20	89	-	-	-	83	-	17
6	60/31	37	44	16	90	-	10	-	90	-	-
66	112/56	56	66	15	93	6	2	3	85	-	4
29	16/9	9	9	9	92	8	-	-	92	-	-
11	55/34	34	37	8	64	36	-	-	64	-	-
17	45/20	24	34	29	66	16	18	-	66	-	-
29	60/36	37	45	18	98	8	3	-	89	-	-
65	510/205	262	227	-15	84	-	-	-	100	-	-
22	455/297	306	407	25	91	-	9	-	91	-	-
49	284/128	140	172	19	115	7	-	-	93	-	-
12	49/20	23	28	18	93	8	28	-	64	-	-
7	57/28	30	36	17	92	6	-	-	94	-	-
11	102/80	81	76	-6	47	2	48	-	50	-	-
44	104/52	53	66	21	92	5	1	-	94	-	-
27				14	86	7	8	0	83	0	2

· JAPAN ·
Investment trusts with at least

Total assets £ million	High/ low pence	Share price pence	NAV pence	Discount (-Premium) %	Gearing	Geographical spread					
						UK	N.America	Japan	Far East	Cont.Europe	Other
55	716/432	468	504	7	80	-	-	100	-	-	-
19	135/93	94	108	14	76	-	-	100	-	-	-
46	170/89	97	104	7	100	-	-	100	-	-	-
177	323/180	184	222	15	87	9	-	91	-	-	-
116	212/149	165	186	11	90	-	5	83	-	12	-
83				11	87	2	1	95	0	2	0

· FAR EAST: INCLUDING JAPAN ·

securities, which include a Japanese content of less than 80%.

Trust	Share price total return			NAV total return			5yr Div growth %	Gross yield %	SS
	1yr	5yrs	10yrs	1yr	5yrs	10yrs			
DRAYTON FAR EASTERN	57.5	247.9	538.5	60.8	209.9	463.4	+109.1	0.9	✓
F & C PACIFIC	61.6	193.8	438.4	69.8	183.2	392.2	-21.8	1.4	✓
FLEMING FAR EASTERN	54.6	189.0	543.4	59.4	170.5	463.0	+50.0	1.2	✓
GOVETT ORIENTAL	54.2	198.7	492.9	57.6	175.4	412.6	-31.2	0.8	✓
MARTIN CURRIE PACIFIC	69.6	235.7	-	68.7	217.9	-	-	0.3	✓
TR FAR EAST INCOME	61.8	-	-	70.7	-	-	-	8.7	✓
THORNTON ASIAN	65.0	-	-	63.5	-	-	-	5.3	✓
AVERAGE	60.6	213.0	503.3	64.4	191.4	432.8	+26.5	2.7	

· FAR EAST: EXCLUDING JAPAN ·

Eastern securities, which exclude a Japanese content.

Trust	Share price total return			NAV total return			5yr Div growth %	Gross yield %	SS
	1yr	5yrs	10yrs	1yr	5yrs	10yrs			
ABTRUST NEW DAWN	54.3	-	-	65.0	-	-	-	0.9	
ABTRUST NEW THAI	48.0	-	-	-	-	-	-	-	
CST EMERGING ASIA	64.8	-	-	71.1	-	-	-	1.3	
DRAYTON ASIA	52.0	-	-	64.5	-	-	-	1.7	✓
EFM DRAGON	58.6	-	-	73.2	-	-	-	-	✓
EFM JAVA*	-	-	-	-	-	-	-	-	✓
FIRST PHILIPPINE*	52.2	-	-	-	-	-	-	-	✓
GARTMORE EMERGING PACIFIC	-	-	-	-	-	-	-	0.4	✓
KOREA-EUROPE	42.1	-	-	61.7	-	-	-	2.3	
KOREA LIBERALISATION	-	-	-	-	-	-	-	-	
PACIFIC ASSETS	50.2	215.3	-	63.3	216.4	-	-	0.8	✓
PACIFIC HORIZON*	50.0	-	-	60.3	-	-	-	-	
PACIFIC PROPERTY	54.6	-	-	60.5	-	-	-	-	
SIAM SELECTIVE*	-	-	-	-	-	-	-	-	
TR PACIFIC	52.1	-	-	66.5	-	-	-	0.6	✓
AVERAGE	52.6	215.3	0.0	65.1	216.4	0.0	+0.0	1.1	

· JAPAN ·

80% of their assets in Japan.

Trust	Share price total return			NAV total return			5yr Div growth %	Gross yield %	SS
	1yr	5yrs	10yrs	1yr	5yrs	10yrs			
BAILLIE GIFFORD JAPAN	65.4	166.8	-	64.3	157.6	-	-	-	✓
BAILLIE GIFFORD SHIN NIPPON	72.5	201.4	-	72.8	207.1	-	-	-	✓
FIRST TOKYO INDEX	55.8	-	-	56.6	-	-	-	-	
FLEMING JAPANESE	57.7	190.6	649.9	60.3	180.6	544.6	-6.3	0.5	✓
GT JAPAN	78.8	269.7	694.1	77.3	242.0	825.6	+100.0	0.9	✓
AVERAGE	66.0	207.1	672.0	66.3	196.8	685.1	+46.9	0.7	

· AUSTRALASIA ·

Investment trusts with at least

Total assets £ million	High/ low pence	Share price pence	NAV pence	Discount (-Premium) %	Gearing	UK	N.America	Japan	Far East	Cont.Europe	Other
7	107/55	56	68	18	-	-	-	-	100	-	-
7				18	0	0	0	0	100	0	0

· EUROPE ·

Investment trusts with at least 80%

Total assets £ million	High/ low pence	Share price pence	NAV pence	Discount (-Premium) %	Gearing	UK	N.America	Japan	Far East	Cont.Europe	Other
25	103/65	67	73	8	82	1	-	-	-	82	11
36	194/133	143	153	7	93	-	-	-	-	100	-
12	53/31	34	40	16	98	19	-	-	-	81	-
67	424/156	157	137	-15	103	6	-	-	-	94	-
38	146/84	98	97	-2	96	1	-	-	-	99	-
-	100/50	54	-	-	-	-	-	-	-	-	-
-	101/57	63	-	-	-	-	-	-	-	-	-
29	100/64	65	72	10	94	-	-	-	-	100	-
137	298/201	211	210	0	98	3	-	-	-	97	-
16	123/78	81	87	7	85	19	1	-	-	80	-
-	105/62	78	-	-	-	-	-	-	-	-	-
-	278/174	188	-	-	-	-	-	-	-	-	-
33	1990/923	1284	1441	11	89	-	-	-	-	100	-
17	112/70	73	75	3	101	-	-	-	-	100	-
26	6025/4200	4450	4663	5	92	-	-	-	-	100	-
24	116/74	77	81	5	78	-	-	-	-	100	-
35	101/87	87	95	9	77	3	-	-	-	97	-
6	41/24	26	31	16	78	50	2	-	-	48	-
18	208/143	143	187	24	25	75	-	-	-	-	25
35				7	86	12	0	0	0	85	2

· FINANCIAL & PROPERTY ·

Investment trusts with at least 80%

Total assets £ million	High/ low pence	Share price pence	NAV pence	Discount (-Premium) %	Gearing	UK	N.America	Japan	Far East	Cont.Europe	Other
100	55/30	32	38	17	92	83	5	1	7	4	-
-	72/45	47	-	-	-	-	-	-	-	-	-
100				17	92	83	5	1	7	4	0

· AUSTRALASIA ·

80% of their assets in Japan.

Trust	Share price total return			NAV total return			5yr Div growth %	Gross yield %	SS
	1yr	5yrs	10yrs	1yr	5yrs	10yrs			
NEW ZEALAND	57.6	-	-	73.9	-	-	-	6.0	
AVERAGE	57.6	0.0	0.0	73.9	0.0	0.0	+0.0	6.0	

· EUROPE ·

of their assets in Continental Europe.

Trust	Share price total return			NAV total return			5yr Div growth %	Gross yield %	SS
	1yr	5yrs	10yrs	1yr	5yrs	10yrs			
ABTRUST NEW EUROPEAN	-	-	-	-	-	-	-	-	
CONTINENTAL ASSETS	75.0	145.8	-	86.5	166.7	-	-	0.1	✓
EUROPEAN PROJECT	65.0	-	-	-	-	-	-	-	
F & C EUROTRUST	79.4	192.1	663.8	75.1	154.1	498.6	+33.8	1.0	✓
F & C GERMANY	-	-	-	-	-	-	-	-	✓
FIRST IRELAND	-	-	-	-	-	-	-	-	
FIRST SPANISH	64.0	-	-	-	-	-	-	1.8	
FLEMING EURO FLEDGELING	-	-	-	-	-	-	-	-	✓
FLEMING UNIVERSAL	74.1	209.0	555.2	78.2	155.9	380.5	+4.9	1.8	✓
GARTMORE EUROPEAN	67.2	135.2	312.2	70.5	112.7	279.2	+31.8	1.4	✓
GERMAN	-	-	-	-	-	-	-	-	
GERMAN SMALLER COMPANIES	73.5	169.3	-	-	-	-	-	0.9	
GREECE FUND	153.4	-	-	158.6	-	-	-	0.3	
MARTIN CURRIE EUROPEAN	-	-	-	-	-	-	-	-	
MEDITERRANEAN FUND	77.2	-	-	-	-	-	-	-	
PARIBAS FRENCH	74.4	-	-	70.5	-	-	-	1.6	
TR EUROPEAN GROWTH	-	-	-	-	-	-	-	1.5	✓
THORNTON PAN EUROPEAN*	-	-	-	-	-	-	-	2.1	
TURKEY TRUST*	-	-	-	-	-	-	-	-	
AVERAGE	80.3	170.3	510.4	87.3	156.0	386.1	+23.5	1.3	

· FINANCIAL & PROPERTY ·

of their assets in Financial & Property.

Trust	Share price total return			NAV total return			5yr Div growth %	Gross yield %	SS
	1yr	5yrs	10yrs	1yr	5yrs	10yrs			
TR PROPERTY	60.7	145.7	339.6	63.6	134.1	291.4	+144.9	6.1	✓
TRUST OF PROPERTY	70.3	106.7	382.6	-	-	-	+233.0	3.4	
AVERAGE	65.5	126.2	361.1	63.6	134.1	291.4	+189.0	4.8	

· COMMODITY & ENERGY ·

Investment trusts with at least 80%

Total assets £ million	High/ low pence	Share price pence	NAV pence	Discount (-Premium) %	Gearing	Geographical spread					
						UK	N.America	Japan	Far East	Cont.Europe	Other
-	115/66	66	-	-	-	-	-	-	-	-	-
17	223/120	130	141	8	91	9	69	-	20	2	-
17				8	91	9	69	0	20	2	0

· TECHNOLOGY ·

Investment trusts with at least

Total assets £ million	High/ low pence	Share price pence	NAV pence	Discount (-Premium) %	Gearing	Geographical spread					
						UK	N.America	Japan	Far East	Cont.Europe	Other
5	42/34	35	41	15	68	84	16	-	-	-	-
156	92/22	22	50	56	308	51	35	7	-	6	1
81				36	188	68	26	4	0	3	1

· SMALLER COMPANIES ·

A majority of investments should each have an equity market capitalisation

Total assets £ million	High/ low pence	Share price pence	NAV pence	Discount (-Premium) %	Gearing	Geographical spread					
						UK	N.America	Japan	Far East	Cont.Europe	Other
12	96/66	67	86	23	95	99	1	-	-	-	-
75	139/96	96	94	-2	130	81	14	3	2	-	-
40	288/218	218	236	8	96	98	1	1	-	-	-
89	92/69	70	82	15	106	57	21	8	3	11	-
7	13/8	8	9	16	93	95	-	5	-	-	-
29	245/160	161	191	16	109	58	29	1	6	6	-
370	232/186	192	235	18	71	69	18	4	4	2	3
21	192/77	77	107	28	194	100	-	-	-	-	-
17	152/97	98	101	3	112	100	-	-	-	-	-
7	105/78	78	84	8	108	97	3	-	-	-	-
34	251/183	183	220	17	80	91	7	-	-	1	1
31	74/55	57	67	16	99	86	3	-	5	6	-
27	117/93	95	98	3	89	100	-	-	-	-	-
22	367/271	273	327	16	107	95	3	-	1	1	-
24	100/84	85	94	10	41	98	2	-	-	-	-

· COMMODITY & ENERGY ·

of their assets in Commodity & Energy.

Trust	Share price total return			NAV total return			5yr Div growth %	Gross yield %	SS
	1yr	5yrs	10yrs	1yr	5yrs	10yrs			
NORTH AMERICAN GAS	63.6	-	-	-	-	-	-	7.6	
PRECIOUS METALS	67.2	124.6	-	67.9	112.6	-	+263.6	2.1	
AVERAGE	65.4	124.6	0.0	67.9	112.6	0.0	+263.6	4.9	

· TECHNOLOGY ·

80% of their assets in Technology.

Trust	Share price total return			NAV total return			5yr Div growth %	Gross yield %	SS
	1yr	5yrs	10yrs	1yr	5yrs	10yrs			
BAILLIE GIFFORD TECHNOLOGY	96.0	116.8	-	85.1	98.6	-	-	-	
TR TECHNOLOGY - ORD	25.1	-	-	31.3	-	-	-	12.1	
AVERAGE	60.6	116.8	0.0	58.2	98.6	0.0	+0.0	12.1	

· SMALLER COMPANIES ·

lower than the average market capitalisation in each geographical area.

Trust	Share price total return			NAV total return			5yr Div growth %	Gross yield %	SS
	1yr	5yrs	10yrs	1yr	5yrs	10yrs			
CLYDESDALE	74.2	-	-	82.1	-	-	-6.0	6.9	✓
DRAYTON ENGLISH & INT	76.3	154.6	465.2	63.4	126.3	314.9	+71.4	4.2	✓
DUNDEE AND LONDON	85.9	138.6	394.7	76.7	120.5	295.4	+122.2	7.3	✓
F & C SMALLER COMPANIES	82.5	166.2	420.3	77.4	147.4	358.7	+76.5	3.2	✓
FIRST CHARLOTTE	72.8	82.6	-	68.9	82.1	-	+300.0	3.6	✓
GLEMING FLEDGELING	71.5	157.0	-	68.6	144.3	353.1	+72.0	3.6	✓
FLEMING MERCANTILE	87.6	170.3	425.0	86.5	161.0	389.4	+90.0	4.3	✓
GRAHAMS RINTOUL	40.2	-	-	50.2	-	-	-	2.6	
LEINWORT SMALLER COMPANIES	70.2	137.1	390.4	61.8	112.0	338.1	+95.7	6.2	✓
LANCASHIRE & LONDON	81.6	129.3	290.8	70.5	111.0	229.3	+85.5	5.0	
LONDON & STRATHCLYDE	76.2	122.5	322.6	76.0	122.4	299.2	+105.7	4.0	✓
LONDON ATLANTIC	82.2	153.1	340.9	78.8	135.5	342.5	+63.8	6.1	
MOORGATE	93.3	203.5	519.5	84.7	186.4	612.2	+166.3	7.3	
NORTH BRITISH CANADIAN	79.5	151.8	344.6	79.9	136.6	370.1	+69.4	6.0	
RIVER & MERC SMALLER COS	-	-	-	-	-	-	-	5.9	

37

· SMALLER COMPANIES ·

A majority of investments should each have an equity market capitalisation

Total assets £ million	High/ low pence	Share price pence	NAV pence	Discount (-Premium) %	Gearing	Geographical spread					
						UK	N.America	Japan	Far East	Cont.Europe	Other
71	240/193	194	204	5	93	67	13	8	2	10	-
13	100/68	68	85	20	96	100	-	-	-	-	-
21	142/110	111	133	17	94	50	19	15	1	15	-
240	158/101	103	122	16	105	69	19	10	-	-	2
-	86/57	59	-	-	-	-	-	-	-	-	-
-	123/93	94	-	-	-	-	-	-	-	-	-
61				13	99	85	8	3	1	3	0

· VENTURE CAPITAL ·

The same rule as for smaller companies, with the added proviso that they have a positive policy of providing

Total assets £ million	High/ low pence	Share price pence	NAV pence	Discount (-Premium) %	Gearing	Geographical spread					
						UK	N.America	Japan	Far East	Cont.Europe	Other
-	298/193	233	-	-	-	-	-	-	-	-	-
25	284/154	154	206	25	92	28	72	-	-	-	-
207	563/367	367	517	29	82	75	19	3	2	1	-
-	301/224	224	-	-	-	-	-	-	-	-	-
10	216/155	155	214	27	87	100	-	-	-	-	-
331	103/43	52	78	34	142	66	12	-	4	15	3
-	33/27	31	-	-	-	-	-	-	-	-	-
37	92/69	69	121	43	83	52	44	3	-	1	-
7	88/40	43	52	18	77	100	-	-	-	-	-
-	108/98	99	-	-	-	-	-	-	-	-	-
-	29/21	21	-	-	-	-	-	-	-	-	-
-	54/29	30	-	-	-	-	-	-	-	-	-
21	345/285	285	345	17	41	98	-	-	-	2	-
-	48/32	32	-	-	-	-	-	-	-	-	-
80	315/218	218	314	31	75	86	4	1	2	7	-
14	72/43	45	59	24	-	100	-	-	-	-	-
-	153/119	119	-	-	-	-	-	-	-	-	-
19	66/38	38	51	27	114	42	-	-	-	58	-
75				28	88	75	15	1	1	8	0

· SMALLER COMPANIES ·

lower than the average market capitalisation in each geographical area.

Trust	Share price total return			NAV total return			5yr Div growth %	Gross yield %	SS
	1yr	5yrs	10yrs	1yr	5yrs	10yrs			
ST ANDREW	87.7	187.6	530.1	77.1	152.8	410.4	+143.5	4.5	✓
SMALLER COMPANIES	-	-	-	-	-	-	-	-	✓
STRATA	80.2	117.0	-	79.5	136.1	-	-	1.6	✓
TR SMALLER COS	68.4	153.7	387.2	71.0	137.7	332.2	+78.9	4.4	✓
THROGMORTON TRUST	72.6	137.3	422.4	-	-	-	+112.0	7.4	
THROGMORTON USM	83.0	-	-	-	-	-	-	4.7	
AVERAGE	77.2	147.6	404.1	66.0	134.1	357.4	+102.9	4.9	

· VENTURE CAPITAL ·

capital for buy-outs, start-ups, etc, and have a "hands-on" approach to management of their investments.

Trust	Share price total return			NAV total return			5yr Div growth %	Gross yield %	SS
	1yr	5yrs	10yrs	1yr	5yrs	10yrs			
CANDOVER	92.1	371.1	-	-	-	-	+949.5	4.0	
CONSOLIDATED VENTURE	55.0	148.4	311.1	65.4	156.4	359.3	-88.2	0.1	✓
DRAYTON CONSOLIDATED	69.0	131.1	320.2	77.9	146.8	290.5	+70.0	6.2	✓
ELECTRA	77.0	178.6	632.2	-	-	-	+64.9	3.6	
ENGLISH & CALEDONIAN	73.9	-	-	75.3	-	-	-	2.6	✓
ENSIGN	51.2	93.0	-	68.5	123.2	-	+85.7	3.4	✓
F & C ENTERPRISE	100.5	132.9	-	-	-	-	+60.0	0.7	✓
GT VENTURE	78.8	-	-	99.5	-	-	-	4.9	✓
GREYFRIARS	53.6	-	-	61.5	-	-	-	18.8	
GROSVENOR DEV CAP	94.3	-	-	-	-	-	-	-	
GR゛ ゛DEV CAP	72.9	-	-	-	-	-	-	1.3	
INDEPENDENT	57.1	-	-	-	-	-	+100.0	1.1	
KLEINWORT DEVELOPMENT	87.5	-	-	91.8	-	-	-	4.0	
LONDON AMERICAN VENTURES	67.0	46.3	-	-	-	-	-	-	
MURRAY VENTURES	73.6	152.4	460.1	86.5	186.2	500.5	+240.0	5.7	✓
RALSTON	66.6	-	-	72.7	-	-	-	6.0	
SUMIT	82.2	-	-	52.5	-	-	-	6.5	
WORTH	56.2	-	-	79.5	-	-	-	0.7	✓
AVERAGE	72.7	156.7	430.9	75.6	153.2	383.4	+185.2	4.4	

Split Capital Trusts

With Winding-Up Dates

Total assets £ million	High/low pence	Share price pence	NAV pence	Discount (-Premium) %	Gearing	Geographical spread					
						UK	N.America	Japan	Far East	Cont.Europe	Other
54	1500/1160	1220	1364	11	102	80	7	6	5	2	-
-	45/40	44	-	-	-	-	-	-	-	-	-
10	238/188	191	213	10	101	100	-	-	-	-	-
10	278/243	243	288	16	-	-	-	-	-	-	-
-	880/690	710	-	-	-	-	-	-	-	-	-
-	475/385	415	-	-	-	-	-	-	-	-	-
15	45/30	35	63	44	168	100	-	-	-	-	-
15	109/98	103	60	-71	-	-	-	-	-	-	-
81	154/84	92	138	34	91	98	2	-	-	-	-
81	118/104	116	61	-89	-	-	-	-	-	-	-
-	88/66	68	-	-	-	-	-	-	-	-	-
-	143/125	126	-	-	-	-	-	-	-	-	-
63	108/55	55	121	55	188	99	1	-	-	-	-
-	97/85	97	-	-	-	-	-	-	-	-	-
-	375/245	265	-	-	-	-	-	-	-	-	-
-	123/97	98	-	-	-	-	-	-	-	-	-
15	29/16	17	30	45	129	-	100	-	-	-	-
15	99/84	87	43	-1	-	-	-	-	-	-	-
17	24/14	18	25	30	177	93	1	-	4	-	2
17	101/86	100	60	-66	-	-	-	-	-	-	-
110	103/70	86	121	29	228	83	14	-	1	-	2
110	107/91	102	59	-74	-	-	-	-	-	-	-
80	75/43	58	115	50	110	93	1	-	2	2	2
80	107/91	99	52	-91	-	-	-	-	-	-	-
278	68/30	45	37	-22	-	95	-	-	-	3	2
278	101/87	99	65	-51	-	-	-	-	-	-	-
27	370/250	290	590	51	-	98	2	-	-	-	-
27	98/85	93	28	-35	-	-	-	-	-	-	-
104	1765/1365	1385	1498	8	97	94	5	1	-	-	-
-	80/61	63	-	-	-	-	-	-	-	-	-
58	157/113	121	135	10	164	94	3	-	1	2	-
-	118/108	110	-	-	-	-	-	-	-	-	-
70				-19	141	87	10	1	1	1	1
95				9	108	54	12	6	13	13	1

Trust		Share price total return			NAV total return			5yr Div growth %	Gross yield %	SS
		1yr	5yrs	10yrs	1yr	5yrs	10yrs			
CITY & COMMERCIAL	- CAP	83.0	194.6	557.1	76.1	149.4	422.9	-	-	
1988 - 01/02/1993	- INC	122.9	221.0	407.9	135.5	341.0	669.9	+114.4	23.8	
ENGLISH NATIONAL	- DEF	84.6	237.2	723.3	84.3	202.4	797.0	+278.5	7.6	✓
No fixed date	- PREF	91.5	219.3	725.0	89.2	178.0	464.1	+105.2	8.7	✓
EQUITY CONSORT	- DEF	88.9	167.3	487.7	-	-	-	+135.7	6.3	
No fixed date	- ORD	97.7	186.3	483.5	-	-	-	+87.5	6.9	
EXMOOR DUAL	- ORD	85.4	-	-	73.4	-	-	-	6.4	
31/08/2001	- INC	104.7	-	-	112.4	-	-	-	12.4	
GENERAL CONSOLIDATED	- CAP	61.4	-	-	54.2	-	-	-	-	
31/12/1997	- INC	114.3	-	-	126.3	-	-	-	11.8	
MEZZANINE CAP & INC	- CAP	81.9	-	-	-	-	-	-	-	
From 01/12/2001	- INC	97.2	-	-	-	-	-	-	15.3	
NEW THROGMORTON (1983)	- CAP	51.9	152.8	-	53.1	117.1	-	-	-	
From 31/03/2008	- INC	113.1	254.0	-	127.0	279.8	-	+196.3	11.1	
RIGHTS & ISSUES	- CAP	74.5	232.4	-	-	-	-	+242.2	3.5	
From 25/07/1991	- INC	84.8	241.8	-	-	-	-	+87.5	9.9	
RIVER & MERC AMERICAN	- CAP	61.1	-	-	73.3	-	-	-	-	
28/02/1999	- INC	96.3	-	-	91.8	-	-	-	12.0	
RIVER & MERC GEARED	- CAP	76.1	-	-	75.2	-	-	-	-	
From 30/09/1999	- INC	112.4	-	-	100.0	-	-	-	10.0	
RIVER & MERCANTILE	- CAP	89.6	-	-	51.8	-	-	-	-	
30/04/2000	- INC	117.3	-	-	121.9	-	-	-	10.3	
RIVER PLATE & GENERAL	- CAP	82.9	-	-	60.1	-	-	-	-	
31/10/1996	- INC	117.7	-	-	140.4	-	-	-	11.5	
SCOTTISH NATIONAL	- CAP	75.0	-	-	23.7	-	-	-	-	✓
30/09/1998	- INC	112.7	-	-	122.7	-	-	-	10.8	✓
THROGMORTON DUAL	- CAP	81.7	-	-	76.4	-	-	-	-	
31/12/1999	- INC	119.0	-	-	96.0	-	-	+133.3	13.2	
TRIPLEVEST	- CAP	80.8	179.2	458.6	76.7	127.2	322.4	-	-	
1987 - 28/02/1991	- INC	114.1	221.6	409.8	148.7	491.1	1105.8	+123.2	40.4	
YEOMAN	- CAP	81.2	-	-	71.3	-	-	-	-	
From 30/09/1992	- INC	113.1	-	-	114.0	-	-	-	16.6	
AVERAGE		92.8	209.0	531.6	91.4	235.8	630.4	+150.4	12.4	
OVERALL AVERAGE		78.2	172.8	498.0	78.5	160.2	426.0	+124.7	6.0	

41

CHAPTER THREE:
ANALYSING THE OPTIONS

With more than 200 investment trust companies to choose from, how do you start picking the right one? The first stage is to sort out which type of trust will best suit your needs. It is here that the AITC's policy of dividing trusts into various categories will help.

Investment trust companies are not free to invest shareholders' money at whim. They must stick to the framework stated in the company's memorandum and articles of association. This will lay down the strategy in a number of areas:

● **Income versus capital growth**

A capital growth trust will aim to increase the capital value of the investments in the portfolio without worrying about yield. That is, it will seek companies which are putting all their resources into growth, rather than paying part of them out to shareholders as dividends.

Income growth trusts will look for companies which are paying dividends, and are likely to continue to do so. Growth and income are not mutually exclusive objectives, though if you are getting an above-average increase in income, then you may well have to sacrifice some measure of capital growth.

There are rather more investment trusts dedicated solely to capital growth than to income. The first investment policy category, UK General, is designed to achieve a balanced return. It contains many of the industry's largest trusts.

The UK Income Growth sector consists of seven trusts and the International Income Sector of just three trusts. The other category we might include among those with an income objective is the seventeen-strong split capital trusts, where the income shareholders are interested in income to the exclusion, or near exclusion, of capital growth.

The rest of the trust categories are wholly growth orientated. Why are there more capital growth trusts than income trusts? The investment trust sector has a long history of providing a growing income for investors. A period of hyper inflation followed by prolonged rising markets resulted in a view that share investments were more suited to capital growth than to the income objective, and that there are greater prospects for capital growth on a portfolio where income is not a main requirement. Although investment trusts can still be a very valuable income investment, especially over the long term, the increasing trend towards specialisation in individual overseas markets where yields overall tend to be low has also caused groups to give less importance to the income objectives. As we have noted this trend may be reversing in the more sober and savings conscious nineties.

A pure growth trust should be regarded as rather more risky than a trust which has an income component. If the markets in which the trusts are invested take a downturn, there will be precious little capital growth, but if the trust invests for income, there will usually be a certain level of return through dividends.

The degree of importance which a trust gives to income can be often spotted by looking at the yield. The income categories will usually have the highest yields, but only in the UK Income Growth category are they uniformly high. In the UK General category they may vary widely. For example in November 1990 they ranged from less than 4% to over 8%. Some trusts in the capital growth categories may have yields which are higher than some Capital and Income growth trusts.

Looking at the categories which specialise in different geographical areas, you can see that Japan and Far East trusts have particularly low yields. This is simply because there are very few companies in these markets which pay out high dividends. Though this is no good to an income investor, it will be suitable for those who do not want additional income because they pay higher rate tax.

The capital growth categories include specialisations by both geographical area and industrial sector. These are likely to be of interest to the larger investor who can afford to hold a spread of different trusts. Investing in a single market carries more risk than dividing up your investment over different markets, so the smaller investor should look at trusts which have broadly spread portfolios.

● Geographical spread

We have already touched on the origins of the industry, which emerged in order to give smaller investors the opportunity of investing abroad. The 'sunrise economy' of the nineteenth century was America, and the original American bias of some trusts is still reflected in their names, even though they may not now be in the North American specialist category, nor have a majority of their portfolios invested in the US.

Stock markets in Japan and the Far East have developed quickly over recent years and most management groups will now have specialist trusts for these markets. The investment trust industry has historically been ahead of the insurance companies and pension funds in building up overseas investment expertise. This is now no longer the case. The large investment institutions nowadays will cover all the world's major markets with their own in-house teams. Many smaller companies are still keen to use investment trusts as a relatively cheap way of harnessing the proven expertise of leading City firms.

Other than those whose objectives limit them to one particular market, most capital growth trusts tend to have well spread portfolios. There are not even very many which invest exclusively in the UK. Income portfolios are likely to be less widely spread. For instance, they will tend to avoid the Japan and Far East markets, where yields are low on ordinary shares. You can get an idea of geographical spread for each trust from the AITC's monthly table.

You will find trusts within the same category have markedly different geographic spreads. This may be caused by an emphasis within the trust's portfolio on a sector which is better represented in some markets than in others. For instance, there is no significant commodities and energy industry in Japan. Also, trusts with a large percentage of smaller companies' shares tend to invest mainly in the UK and North America, because these markets are the best researched and have reasonably liquid second tier or junior stock markets. More often it simply reflects trust managers' different views on the relative attractiveness of world markets.

● Unquoted investments

The investment trust portfolio objectives include policy with regard to unquoted companies, that is, those whose shares are not listed on a stock exchange. A few trusts specialise in unquoted companies. Many more have a small proportion of such investments.

An unquoted, or unlisted, company is one in whose shares there are no dealings on any organised stock market. With such companies shares are bought by private arrangement between the company, or an agent who is raising capital on behalf of the company, and the investor. Share deals arranged in this way may be few and far between. As there will be relatively few investors prepared to undertake this kind of investment selling stock will not be easy. For this reason investors tend to find themselves 'locked in' to unquoted investments until the company concerned becomes large enough to get a stock market quotation. Once this happens, the shares are much more freely marketable, and the investor can sell – usually at a very considerable profit on the price at which he bought.

There are many different kinds of unquoted company. They may be private family firms which have been running for years, and have never sought a quotation because the owners wanted to keep the stock under their control. They may be very young companies: for instance, ones which have not yet even started trading, but consist of an entrepreneur looking for some capital to put a business idea into practice, or those which are already operating but need additional capital to finance development.

The business of providing finance for very young companies is known as venture capital. If the company is already in business, but is looking for a further injection of cash, the investment comes under the heading of development capital.

This sort of financing is obviously very risky. A very large percentage of start-ups fail, and the future of most developing companies is by no means certain. Whereas in a portfolio of blue chip companies a failure would be very rare, among unquoted companies generally the percentage can be high.

The incentive for investing in unquoted companies is the very high return which can be produced on the investments which are successful, and the point of doing it through an investment trust is that the trust can afford to hold a percentage of unquoteds along with a more broadly spread portfolio. It can also afford to wait for them to mature, and it has the expertise to choose and monitor the companies concerned.

Since investments in unquoted companies are undertaken largely on a private and ad hoc basis, it is hard for the ordinary individual to get in touch with companies seeking venture capital. The costs and difficulties of doing so mean the process is usually not worth while. For instance, to invest in US unquoted stocks you would probably pay more in bank charges for the bank to collect the dividends than you would get in yield from the investments.

Unquoted companies are not widely open to public scrutiny in the same way as those which have a quotation. They do not have to publish the same amount of information about themselves, and finding out about them is literally a matter of going along and asking. An investment trust manager looking at unquoted companies will probably not start out from quite such a basic level. The company concerned may be introduced to him by a regional stockbroker who knows the company locally, or who specialises in this type of company.

However, if the trust links its fortunes to those of the company by investing, the manager will want to keep a very close eye on its progress. A condition of the investment may be that the company reports monthly to the trust managers, and that the management group's unquoted specialist sits on the company's board of directors. Even more basic involvement in the day-to-day running of the company might be called for in the event of a crisis, though trust managers will do their best to avoid this, as the investment then begins to take up too much management time.

As it is not listed on a formal market, one of the problems of an unquoted company is that there is no public source of valuation. In other words, there is no daily price arrived at through market dealings, so knowing how much the investment is worth is a matter of informed calculation on the part of the trust managers. Companies valued in this way are described in the trust's report and accounts as being 'at directors' valuation'.

The fortunes of an unquoted company may change radically between annual reports, so directors' valuations may be subject to considerable adjustments. If shares in an unquoted company change hands during the year, the trust manager will get an outside view on what his holding is currently worth, but the holding may only appear to have performed really well when a quotation is imminent. It is hard for unquoted holdings to look good when equity markets are rising strongly, because the shares simply cannot be revalued in a way which keeps pace with the market.

Unquoted companies in the UK have also started to look very expensive over the last few years thanks to the advent of the government's Business Expansion Scheme, under which many new issues of shares and specialist funds have been launched, linked to generous tax incentives to the private investor to put his money into young companies.

● Currencies

The importance of currencies is inescapable in a largely overseas investment medium, because changes in foreign exchange values can affect the performance of a portfolio just as much as the behaviour of markets.

The figures below show how market indices in various countries round the world grew over the whole of 1986. The left hand column shows the percentage growth in local currency. The right hand column gives the same growth figure adjusted to sterling – that is, divided by a factor representing the change in exchange rate between sterling and the relevant currency.

Market movements in 1990 adjusted for currencies

	% change during 1990	
	local	*£ adjusted*
US: Dow Jones Industrial	−4.3	−20.1
Japan: Tokyo New Stock Exchange	−39.8	−46.7
Australia: All Ordinaries	−22.4	−36.7
Hong Kong: Hang Seng Bank	6.6	−10.9
France: CAC General	−24.1	−27.9
Germany: Commerzbank	−22.3	−26.6
Italy: Banca Commerciale	−24.9	−29.4

Source: County NatWest WoodMac.

As you can see, the changes in currencies had quite an impact on performance. In most cases the decline for the UK investor was increased by comparison to the return to the local investor.

Where the sterling-adjusted performance is better than local performance the pound fell against the currency concerned. Where the sterling-adjusted performance is worse than local performance, sterling rose against the currency, as was the case against the world's major currencies in 1990.

Example:
£1 = $1
    £100 shares = $100
£1 strengthens to $2
    Same $100 in shares is now worth £50 ($100 ÷ 2)
£1 falls to 50c
    Same $100 in shares is now worth £200 ($100 ÷ 0.5)

The example assumes that the dollar value of the shares remains the same throughout. If the dollar value of the investment goes down (that is, if the US market falls), a fall in sterling will counteract the effect and a rise in sterling will add to the effect. If the US market rises, a fall in sterling will enhance the gain, and a rise in sterling will reduce it.

Investors would be completely at the mercy of currency gains and losses if it were not for the process known as hedging. Hedging describes any of a number of different currency transactions designed to neutralise the effects of shifting exchange rates. At its simplest and most cumbersome, hedging is achieved by the use of back-to-back loans. The trust will use its investments in the US as security for a dollar loan, which matches the US asset with a US liability, and effectively removes the currency risk. An investment trust can also use much more sophisticated financial futures, as well as foreign currency loans. In fact, by the use of loans, a trust can effectively turn itself into a dollar investor investing in Japan, or an Italian lira investor investing in Germany.

CHAPTER FOUR:
MEASURING RETURN

As we have already seen in chapter one, investment trusts have an impressive performance record. They have in recent years beaten deposit investments like building society and bank accounts by a very wide margin, as Table One shows. Not every single trust is a top performer, of course, but one of the most striking aspects of the industry's success is that

Table One: Investment trusts compared with other investments

	5 years	10 years
INVESTMENT TRUST		
UK (general)	175.02	474.68
International (capital growth)	173.37	464.40
UNIT TRUST SECTOR:		
UK General	170.19	496.13
International	136.49	336.76
BUILDING SOCIETY		
(high interest)	155.54	238.74
BANK DEPOSIT ACCOUNT (gross)	132.20	197.29
FTA ALL-SHARE INDEX	174.09	471.84

Source: Micropal, A.I.T.C. and UTA.

Note: Figures show results of £100 invested over 5 years or 10 years to 31.12.1990
Investment trust figures are on an offer-to-offer basis as are the unit trust figures.
Figures for both investment trusts and unit trusts refer to the average return.

the average trust has performed very strongly compared to the movement in stock markets around the world.

The Association of Investment Trust Companies publishes monthly figures which illustrate the different aspects of investment trust performance. Two main types of performance are shown: the changes in share price and net asset value. The share price hardly needs an explanation. It is what you pay for your shares, and how they are valued by the market from day to day. It is quoted in the daily papers, so it is easy to look up. The net asset value (NAV) is the current value of the assets backing each ordinary share issued by an investment trust. It is a net figure because it is arrived at after deducting from the total value of the assets all the liabilities due to creditors and all capital with a prior claim to repayment.

Net asset values are quoted in the AITC's published monthly table and are shown in pence per share, so that they can be compared directly with market prices. This enables investors to calculate and monitor the movement in the level of discount. However, it must be pointed out that a monthly calculation is only useful as a guide and cannot be compared with the daily statistics produced by specialist stockbrokers and used extensively by professional investors.

The AITC also produces figures which make a distinction between performance and total return. Performance is simply the change, whether in the trust's market price or in its net asset value per share, over a given period.

Total return, on the other hand, provides a measure of both capital and income performance combined. This is done by assuming that dividends paid on shares are reinvested immediately in buying more shares in that company. Share price total returns are calculated using the market price for 'buying', net asset value total return uses the net asset value per share.

What the AITC figures show are 'results of £100 invested over different periods of time to the end of the specified month'. So, for example, if a performance figure for five years is 380.00 this means £100 invested five years ago would now be worth £380. In other words, it has increased in value by £280. Of course, if you decided to sell your shares, you would have to deduct your broker's commission from this figure.

But what is the purpose of quoting two types of return? The first, share price, enables an investor to compare one company with another, even though they may have different divident policies. The second, based on net asset values, helps us to judge the effectiveness of different managements, by seeing how much better, relatively, one has increased both asset value and dividends over another. Total return figures will always be slightly higher than performance figures, the difference representing the level of dividends paid.

How have they performed?

Apart from looking at performance in isolation, there are a number of measures we can use to put the record of investment trusts into perspective. The industry is normally viewed against a UK stock market index – commonly the FT Actuaries All-Share Index. This index is the 'average' of how the UK market as a whole behaves, and is generally regarded as a tough yardstick to beat.

The investment trust average has had a job to beat the FTA All-Share, though it has generally done so over the longer term. Of course, the trust sector average includes many trusts which are largely or wholly invested outside the UK market, so the comparison is not entirely scientific. The same can be said of the Morgan Stanley Capital International World Index, which the trust sector average has outperformed during the whole period, by a wide and increasing margin.

The average UK trust has also been an excellent hedge against inflation, staying ahead of the Retail Prices Index for almost the whole of the ten years shown in the table, and more than doubling the growth in the index over the whole period.

There is, of course, a lot of difference in performance between the top and bottom trusts in the sector, but the average trust holds up against the index so well, that investors should see good worthwhile resuts even if their trust is not a top performer.

Table Two: Performance comparisons

31st December 1990 Average Performance

	One Year	Five Years	Ten Years
INVESTMENT TRUSTS			
International: general	78.2	172.8	498.0
International: capital growth	82.4	179.3	556.0
International: income growth	85.4	174.1	553.9
UK: general	84.7	169.4	484.7
UK: capital growth	85.1	175.4	648.0
UK: income growth	93.5	193.1	705.2
High Income	77.3	141.8	273.5
North America	66.4	112.3	276.0
Far East including Japan	60.6	213.0	503.3
Far East excluding Japan	52.6	215.3	–
Japan	66.0	207.1	672.0
Australasia	57.6	–	–
Europe	80.3	170.3	510.4
Financial & Property	65.5	126.2	361.1
Commodity & Energy	65.4	123.6	–
Technology	60.6	116.8	–
Smaller Companies	77.2	147.6	404.1
Venture Capital	72.7	156.7	430.9
Split Capital	92.8	209.0	531.6
Unit Trusts (Offer to Offer)	79.6	153.3	401.5
Unit Trusts (Offer to Bid)	75.1	144.0	377.4
INDEX PERFORMANCE			
RPI	109.7	135.5	187.1
Building Society Investment	111.4	155.7	238.9
FTA - All Share	89.0	176.7	493.6
S & P Composite	80.2	133.0	404.4
Tokyo New Stock Exchange	53.5	187.0	699.1
MS Capital International World	69.4	147.9	458.2

Note: The figures above show the comparative return to the investor of a theoretical £100 over various periods, adjusted to include reinvested income. Where averages are given, these are calculated on an arithmetic basis. For split-capital trusts, the average is for capital & income shares combined. Overseas indices have been adjusted for the effect of exchange rate movements.
Source: County NatWest, WoodMac (and *Micropal)

Although the average investment trust may beat the relevant index, there are no guarantees about the level of return. The uncertainties of equity markets are one reason why investment trusts really should be regarded as a long-term investment and should form part of a properly balanced portfolio.

Dividend performance

So far, all the figures we have looked at have shown the capital growth possibilities of investment trusts. There is, however, another and very important form of return: the dividend. Investment trusts have an excellent record as providers of rising dividends, Chart One shows.

This element of producing a rising income should always be kept in mind by income investors when choosing their investments. A building society deposit may offer a higher initial yield but not the prospect of growth. Trust managers seek to provide a rising income, and because the capital value of the underlying investment also rises, dividends on investment trusts can increase so as to offer a return well in excess of an interest-bearing investment.

The yield quoted on an investment trust is calculated by showing the last year's dividend as a percentage of the current share price. It is therefore an indication of the return you would get if you bought shares today. If you bought shares some time ago, when the price was lower, the yield you are getting on your original cost will be higher than the current yield.

A simple example illustrates the point. Suppose you invest £100 in an investment trust with a yield of 4%. In the first year, you will get £4. After three years, the value of your investment has gone up to £150. The current yield, still at 4%, means you will now get £6 in dividends (£150 × 4%). If you take £6 as a percentage of your original £100 investment, you will see you are now getting 6% – half as much again as the current quoted yield.

As a result of this rising dividend effect, investment trusts can be an excellent hedge against inflation.

Chart One: Investment Trust Dividend Growth
(FT Investment Trust Index Dividends)

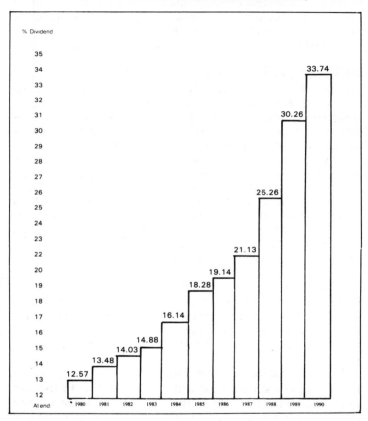

% Dividend

1980	12.57
1981	13.48
1982	14.03
1983	14.88
1984	16.14
1985	18.28
1986	19.14
1987	21.13
1988	25.26
1989	30.26
1990	33.74

At end

In sum

The main strengths of the investment trust sector are consistency of performance, and very good returns not only from the top trusts, but from the average trusts as well. The more general trusts have a steadier record that those which confine themselves to a particular market. The specialist trusts are more vulnerable

55

in terms of performance to changes in fortunes, though they may produce excellent returns over some periods − as in the Japan sector in the eighties.

Trusts have been a good hedge against inflation, both for protecting the investor's capital, and providing a rising income, though income investors will have to wait some years before they see yields in excess of those on the building society. This underlines the fact that investment trusts must be regarded as a long-term investment. Like all share investments, they tend to reflect the movements of stock markets, and returns in the short term may be vulnerable to market fluctuations. It is over the longest periods that investment trusts show the best comparative returns with non-risk deposits.

CHAPTER FIVE:
BUYING AT A DISCOUNT

There are two main measures of investment trust performance: share price and net asset value. Net asset value indicates the underlying paper value of the portfolio of investments held by the trust. There will almost always be a difference between the share price and the net asset value just as there is between the share price of a trading company and the net assets per share as stated in the accounts. This difference is known as the discount if the share price is below the net asset value or the premium if it is above. Most investment trust shares are traded at a discount.

The discount or premium is the difference between the share price and the net asset value, expressed as a percentage of the net asset value. In other words, if the net asset value is 100, and the share price is 80, the discount is 20%. If the price moves up to 110, and the net asset value stays at 100, the trust's shares have moved to a 10% premium.

The main point to remember is that trust share prices are fixed by supply and demand rather than by a pricing formula linked to the value of their portfolio. Therefore, to a shareholder, his interest in the underlying assets of his investment trust shares does not have the same value as the market price of those shares.

The principle of supply and demand means that if there are more buyers than sellers in the market, the share price will go up and vice versa. Good management performance, leading to an increase in net asset value, is not the only thing which makes investors want to buy shares. Likewise, poor performance is not the only thing that makes them want to sell.

Investors may, for instance, decide that a certain market is out of favour. There will then be more sellers than buyers in that particular market, and share prices of trusts which are heavily invested there will fall across the board, though their net asset performance record may be strong. Discounts will tend to widen when markets are felt to be at a peak, or when they are falling, and to narrow when they are expected to rise.

Though it invests in a wide portfolio of shares, an investment trust is also a share in its own right, and has its own characteristics which will affect its price independently of movements in the value of its investment portfolio. It is quoted on the UK stock market, and will therefore respond to overall UK market movements, even if its investments are largely overseas. It may be the subject of bid speculation, which could cause a very strong swing in the share price without a change in the actual value of its assets. The market's perception of the trust's management may alter resulting in the share price moving independently of any change in asset values.

Apart from supply and demand, another reason for the existence of the discount is the distancing effect between the shareholder and the shares in the portfolio. Though the net assets attributable to your shares may have a value of £100, you cannot get your hands on that amount, because what you own is a share in the investment trust company itself, not a direct interest in its assets.

A shareholder can only realise the net asset value of his shares, or something near it, if the trust is taken over or liquidated. The portfolio is then sold, but the notional net asset value will be reduced by:

● the administrative and dealing costs of liquidation

● the difference between the mid-market prices used for calculation the net asset value of the underlying assets and the lower bid prices at which those assets are actually sold

● the effect on the price of a large tranche of shares coming onto the market from the trust's holdings, as the sale of a large amount of shares can, by the laws of supply and demand, make the price fall

● particularly where unquoted shares are concerned, estimated values may not tally with what can actually be realised in the event of a sudden sell-off.

Discount strategy

We have looked at what the discount *is*. The next question

Table One: How the discount varies

Category	Discounts %		
	1990	1989	1988
All Trusts	15.1	13.8	19.1
Non-Specialist	14.4	15.6	20.3
Income Growth	9.1	14.0	15.2
High Income	−2.8	8.6	n/a
Capital Growth			
North America	16.8	9.9	16.8
Far East	14.2	3.2	12.3
Japan	13.7	10.2	11.6
Europe	4.0	−3.2	14.7
Technology	33.5	34.5	34.5
Venture Capital	29.5	17.6	20.1

Source: County NatWest WoodMac.

is whether it is good for the investor. The discount is quoted as an advantage in buying investment trusts. What puzzles many investors is that, though you may be getting extra assets for your money, if your shares are still at the same level of discount when you sell, then you have had no apparent benefit.

In fact there are two ways in which you may benefit from the discount. The first is invisible: because the securities in the portfolio are worth more than the share price you paid, you have extra assets working to produce income. It is as if you had put £80 into the building society, but were actually getting interest on £100.

Secondly, the discount is always changing. You can see from Table One how various discounts for investment trust sectors moved up and down over 1990 and 1989. If you buy shares on a high discount and sell on a low discount, you will be accentuating the effect of any increase, or negating any decline, in the net asset value. The same is true in reverse. If the discount widens while you are holding your shares, the market price will either have fallen more sharply than the underlying asset value, or will not have reflected fully any increase in value.

Twists of fortune

During 1990 there were some striking movements in discount for trusts investing in the Far East. However, overall the discount movements have been less dramatic than in the past as the market for investment trust shares has broadened. During most of the seventies, discounts ranged between 25% and 40% but these have been edging down recently despite the bearish tone in world stock markets. The new era of the nineties should see discounts settling around the 10% to 18% range.

All investment trust shareholders should obviously be aware of the discount, though short term investers will have to pay much more attention to it than those who want to buy shares and stay with them long term. An investor who holds shares over, say, five years, should not be badly affected by discount movement. The more speculative investor, hoping to use changes in discount levels to enhance his dealing profits, will have to pay much more attention to short-term movements.

Herd instinct

It is worth remembering that investment trust shareholders are largely institutions, who tend to move as a herd. This is why sharp discount movements sometimes occur across whole sectors, and can catch the small investor out. If you are a short-term investor, you should watch markets carefully and take action early if you see signs of change. Otherwise, it may be best to hold on and ride out the discount cycle.

Equally, a good quality sector which has gone out of favour with the institutions may present buying opportunities. In the example we give above, an investor buying Far East trust shares at more than 14% discount would have enhanced his growth possibilities in a market which is unlikely to stay in the doldrums for very long.

Is the best strategy then to go for the trust with the highest discount you can find? Not necessarily. As the table shows, different sectors have different discount patterns. For example, a continuing, very high discount will usually indicate a major problem: The sector may be facing a long period of restructuring or difficult trading conditions. This may occur with highly specialised trusts investing in sectors like commodities and technology, which are capable of prolonged troughs in popularity.

By going for the highest discount you can find, you are speculating on a dramatic upturn in the trust's fortunes. This may occur through the trust improving its performance or being taken over – but you can't bank on that happening. You may be locking yourself into a dismal performance record.

If there is an obvious reason for a high discount – such as the case of the Far East, where a strong market is temporarily out of favour – there is much more chance that the discount will move in your favour sooner rather than later.

The future for discounts

Though discounts have traditionally been one of the striking features of investment trusts, it looks increasingly as if their role is becoming less important.

In the 70s, the average discount for the whole investment trust sector veered between 40% and almost 10%. However, in the early 1980s, the spread was more like 30% to 20% and over the last five years the variation has been reduced to a range of about 25% to 18%.

The reason must be put down largely to increasing takeover activity. If trusts remain at a high discount, they will be swallowed up. Trusts which tend to stay at constant high discounts are the general trusts, where institutional dealing in the shares may be proportionately less than specialist trusts. General trusts are vulnerable to predators because their portfolios of mainstream shares are easier to realise. The numbers of such trusts has been reduced by takeover activity in the last few years, reducing the average discount for the sector.

61

With increased interest in the investment trust sector on the part of the investing public, there will be a greater degree of attention given to investment trust performance. This should stimulate managements to perform better and so narrow discounts still further.

CHAPTER SIX:
TOP GEAR FOR PROFIT

Gearing is one of those technical terms that sounds complicated but is actually quite easy to grasp. It is used in a number of different ways in the investment world, sometimes rather loosely. The essential idea it conveys, though, is that of putting into an investment an element such as borrowing whose effect on the return will be proportionately greater than its own cost.

For example, when you use a mortgage for a house purchase, as most of us do, you are actually introducing gearing into the process. Suppose you have a £40,000 mortgage on a house whose purchase price is £60,000. The £20,000 deposit you have to put down is equal to one third of the price, the mortgage to two thirds.

Now let's say the value of the house doubles in ten years to £120,000. Ignoring the interest you have to pay, and looking only at the capital growth on your investment, your original £20,000 deposit has turned into an asset worth £80,000, i.e. the difference between the new house value of £120,000 and the mortgage of £40,000. So your deposit has quadrupled in value while the house price has only doubled. This effect is what gearing is all about.

In an investment trust what is meant by gearing is simply the ability of the company to supplement its resources by borrowing. When it is first set up, the investment trust's resources consist of cash which the shareholders have invested – in other words, its capital. Gearing enters the scene when an investment trust looks outside its circle of shareholders to raise additional money which it then invests. The two most popular ways of raising this extra cash are by issuing loan stock and raising foreign currency loans, particularly to finance overseas investment. The aim is to invest the additional funds at a greater profit than the cost of the borrowings. From a shareholder's point of view, it means there is more money working on his behalf, which, if wisely invested, should add up to bigger profits.

Nitty gritty

Let's look at the nitty gritty of how gearing works. Though you'll see a lot of figures coming up, they are no more complicated than the mortgage example which we used earlier.

Gearing affects both the capital and income return to the ordinary shareholder in an invesment trust. It has the effect of enhancing capital gains, but it also exaggerates losses. So a highly geared trust is an excellent prospect in a rising market, but extra risky in a falling market.

If the market continues to rise, the effect of gearing becomes weaker, unless borrowings are increased, because the borrowings represent a declining percentage of the total portfolio. Conversely, the effect of gearing in a falling market gets progressively stronger, though there are steps managers can take to reduce this effect.

Example One: Top Gear Trust

Structure of trust

	£
£20m 10¼% debenture (i.e. loan) stock	20,000,000
£100m ordinary shares	100,000,000
Initial value of portfolio	120,000,000

Net asset value per ordinary share = £1

Top Gear Trust after five years:

	£
Value of portfolio	240,000,000
Less debenture	20,000,000
Attributable to ordinary shares	220,000,000

Net asset value per ordinary shares = £2.20

a) In rising market

Now for some examples of gearing. The figures at Example One show the capital structure of an imaginary investment trust, at the start of its life. There are 100 million £1 shares in issue and in addition the trust has borrowed £20 million. The initial total value of the portfolio is £120 million. The net asset value per share is £1.00.

After five years the trust's portfolio has doubled in value to £240 million. After deducting £20 million which will be needed to repay the loan, the shareholders are left with £220 million representing the total value of the ordinary shares – a net asset value, in other words, of £2.20 per share, compared to £1 per share at the start of the trust's life. The portfolio has increased by 100%, but the net asset value of the ordinary shares has grown by 120%.

Example Two simply repeats the exercise, looking at the trust after it has doubled in value again. The gearing effect still works, but you can see that this time it only gives an increase of 109% to the net asset value of the ordinary shares, compared to a 100% portfolio increase. In investment jargon, you will see this described as 'the gearing running out'. It simply means that as the borrowing accounts for a decreasing percentage of the money invested, the extra fillip to profits is reduced accordingly.

Example 2: Top Gear Trust after ten years

	£
Value of portfolio	480,000,000
Less debenture	20,000,000
Attributable to ordinary shares	460,000,000

Net asset value per ordinary share = £4.60

b) In falling market

The value of the portfolio declines by 40% to £72 million and, after taking away the value of the debenture, there is only 52p in net asset value to each ordinary share. In other words, the net asset value has been reduced by 48%, compared to a market fall of only 40%.

Example Three: Top Gear Trust in falling market

	£
Value of portfolio	72,000,000
Less debenture	20,000,000
Attributable to ordinary shares	52,000,000

Net asset value per ordinary share = 52p

If you can bear to look, Example Four shows this sad state of affairs continuing, with the market down a further 33%, and the net asset value down by 46%.

Example Four: Top Gear Trust goes on falling

	£
Value of portfolio	48,240,000
Less debenture	20,000,000
Attributable to ordinary shares	28,240,000

Net asset value per ordinary share = 28p

In practice, a market fall as severe as that shown in our examples occurs very rarely, and managers would certainly take steps to reduce the effect of the gearing on a trust as the index went down. All our examples assume the level of gearing was not changed, whatever the market did.

c) Income effect

Our final two examples are happier. They show the income effect of gearing on an ordinary shareholder's dividends. Since the borrowings in the portfolio increase the amount of underlying investments, they logically also increase the amount of dividend income coming into the trust to be passed on to the ordinary shareholder. In contrast, the trust pays a fixed interest charge to the debenture stock holder which is deducted from the trust's income.

In Example Five we have assumed that the portfolio has been invested to produce a fairly modest 3.5% yield in the first year, which is £4,200,000 on the total portfolio. From this, the 10¼% interest is paid on the £20,000,000 debenture, leaving income of £2,150,000 for the ordinary shareholder, or 2.1p per share.

Example Five

Portfolio invested to yield 3.5%

	Yr 1 £
Income from portfolio (3.5% × £120,000,000)	4,200,000
Less debenture interest (10¼% × £20,000,000)	2,050,000
Gross income attributable to the 100,000,000 ordinary shares	2,150,000
Dividend per share	2.1p

Example Six: five years later

	Yr 5 £
Income from portfolio (3.5% × 240,000,000)	8,400,000
Less debenture interest (10¼%× £20,000,000)	2,050,000
Gross income attributable to the 100,000,000 ordinary shares	6,350,000
Dividend per share	6.3p

After five years, looking back at the capital growth pattern in example two, the income, like the portfolio, has doubled. After repayment of the debenture interest, £6,350,000, or 6.3p per share, is left for the ordinary shareholder. In other words, the dividend to shareholders has increased by 200% compared to a 100% increase in portfolio income.

Example Seven assumes an increase in yield to 5.0% in year five, again assuming the trust has doubled in value. This gives us total income of £9,950,000 for the ordinary shareholders after deduction of the debenture interest – 9.95p per share. Shareholders' income has risen by 374%, roughly double the increase in the total income on the portfolio.

67

Example Seven

Yield on portfolio rises to 5% in year 5

	Yr 5 £
Income from portfolio (5% × £240,000,000)	12,000,000
Less debenture interest (10¼% × £20,000,000	2,050,000
Gross income attributable to the 100,000,000 ordinary shares	9,950,000
Dividend per share	9.95p

So gearing can increase both the net asset value of the trust and its income if the value of the trust is increasing. However, as the total portfolio grows in size, the effect of the gearing 'runs out' or decreases. Worse, in a falling market gearing exaggerates portfolio losses. The level of gearing, or whether to have any borrowings at all, is one of the decisions the managers have to revise frequently.

Gearing can be increased without difficulty either through loans or further loan stock issues. It is also possible to reduce the level of gearing on a trust, or 'de-gear'. There are several ways of doing this, but the simplest is to keep a percentage of the portfolio in cash. In other words, not to invest some of the borrowings.

If a bear (or falling) market was anticipated, one would in any case expect a higher percentage of the portfolio to be in cash. Managers are generally cautious, though, about moving large percentages of the portfolio into cash, in case the market rises instead. If this were to happen, a manager holding a high percentage of cash would lose out in performance, and may find it hard to buy back into the market again at worthwhile prices. In any case, a qualifying investment trust is expected to be invested mainly in shares.

Some industry experts argue that investment trusts have not made enough use of gearing in recent years. Gearing was generally higher twenty years ago, but after more than a decade of rising markes the level of gearing has been reduced. This is a pity: as we have seen, a period of rising markets is just the time when a high level of gearing can dramatically increase profits for investors.

Cost effective

Of course, it is not as simple as that. If all managers were given an advance schedule of bull and bear market periods, it would be easy to get gearing levels right. Unfortunately, life isn't like that, and managers have to rely on informed guesswork. No one would thank them for introducing high levels of gearing just as markets had peaked.

An investment trust manager also needs the right revenue conditions in order to borrow – that is, he needs to be able to pay the required interest rate from the trust's income. The circumstances in which gearing is most appropriate are where a trust has the possibility of increasing the income on its investments sufficiently to meet the cost of borrowing *and* pay out the expected dividend to shareholders, or where its income is in any case high enough to permit further borrowing.

As the examples indicate, the interest on a trust's borrowings is met out of the income generated by the portfolio, and therefore reduces the amount available to pay out as dividends to shareholders. If gearing were suddenly increased, there would be a fall in dividends. However, investment trusts, especially the older, very large general trusts, traditionally paid out a higher income each year. Shareholders in such trusts would not welcome a drop in their accustomed dividend. This situation may in some cases be a constraint on managers who would like to increase gearing. With rising interest rates, trusts may also find the cost of borrowing too high.

In practice, loan stocks with a fixed rate of return have become less attractive in recent years as interest rates have settled on a higher plane. To launch a new loan stock now would require a high interest rate 'coupon', and many trusts feel they can't afford this – hence the tendency to switch to gearing through currency loans.

Future policy

It is possible in the future that if investment trust managers want to raise gearing levels, accompanied by a drop in dividend, they may make clear to shareholders that they are adopting a policy of varying dividends to allow for changes in gearing requirements. This in turn may gradually result in a shift in shareholders' attitudes to a point where more emphasis is given to capital growth rather than dividend income.

Looking at the AITC's monthly investment table, you can see that the higher levels of gearing are to be found in the Split Capital and Venture Capital sectors. Gearing levels on the big generalist trusts in the capital and income growth category tend to be fairly low. Since gearing adds an additional element of risk to investment trusts it appears at the time of writing that when the Securities and Investment Board relaxes its rules on the marketing of investment trust it will restrict the new liberal regulations to trusts with no gearing.

CHAPTER SEVEN:
CAPITAL AND LOAN STRUCTURE

In this chapter we shall look at the different classes of stocks and shares available. Probably the main investment of interest to the private investor is the ordinary share, but all aspects of investment trust structure have been covered in some detail because certain features may offer interesting opportunities for the more experienced investor.

Investment trusts may raise any of a number of different types of capital. The main distinction to be drawn is between equity capital and loan stock. Equity capital represents a share in the company itself, and shareholders, receive the benefit of any capital growth, plus a dividend, which in some cases may be small, and which is not guaranteed . Loan stock, as the name implies, is a loan to the company, not a share in it. The important thing with this type of stock is the guarantee of a fixed return.

The different classes of shares can be ranked according to the degree of risk involved. In this context risk reflects the order of priority the investor receives in the creditors' queue in the event of a company being wound up. Using this definition, the lenders to the company – the loan stock holders – rather than the owners of the company – the shareholders – are in the best position. Debenture stock is the least risky, followed by unsecured loan stock. After these in the pecking order come preference shares, ordinary shares and warrants.

However, there should be little immediate risk of a trust being wound up if it is well run. So for most investors security in the event of winding up is not the most important consideration.

Equity Capital

● Ordinary shares

On paper, these sound like the most risky type of capital to buy. They are at the bottom of the creditors' queue in the event of the company being wound up, and nothing about them is guaranteed. Their capital value will rise and fall reflecting demand, and their income can rise, fall, or even disappear altogether.

In practice ordinary shares have been by far the most attractive type of investment for several decades now, due to a series of strongly rising equity markets. Capital values have increased steadily, producing very good returns, and investment trusts have established an excellent record of providing rising dividends. In many trusts, it would be regarded as a major disaster if dividends fell, let alone if they were not paid altogether.

As an investor you need a measured attitude to the risks of ordinary shares in investment trusts. You should not invest on the assumption that ordinary shares are bound to offer uninterrupted steady growth. In a sharply falling stock market, there is no doubt that they will do badly. Capital values will fall, and dividends may be reduced.

You can protect yourself against this possibility by various means: spreading your investments across various markets; having a percentage of your money in interest-bearing rather than capital growth investments; regarding your equity investments as long term, so that you do not find yourself obliged to sell your shares when markets are low; and moving more of your money into guaranteed investments as the time approaches to realise your capital – for instance, in the last five years before retirement.

Provided you do not have to sell your investment trust shares during a severely depressed market, you should not be put off investing due to fear of falling stock markets. Those who put their money into equities in 1970 and sold their shares in 1985 did very well, even though they had to ride out the extraordinarily severe stock market crash of the mid-seventies.

As well as the financial returns they offer, ordinary shares also give certain rights. Shareholders have a right to vote at the company's annual general meeting, giving them some say in how the company runs its affairs. Of course, someone with a few hundred shares does not have much voice. The most influential shareholders are the institutions who hold large percentages of a trust's equity. The AITC Investment Trust Year Book lists shareholders who hold more than 5% of the capital of each trust. These are the organisations – pension funds, insurance companies and the like – who really have the final say when it comes to deciding on issues like takeovers or unitisations. Apart from voting rights, shareholders may also enjoy benefits when it comes to new issues. There are two types of issue the shareholder should know about:

a) Rights issues

A rights issue is simply a way for any company to raise more capital. When there is a rights issue, existing ordinary shareholders are offered the chance to buy more shares, depending on the number of shares they hold already. These are offered at a fixed price, normally substantially below the market price. A one-for-one rights issue means you are being offered one new share for each share you hold. A four-for-one issue would mean four new shares for each existing one, and so on. You do not have to take up the rights issue, and your decision will depend on whether you feel the future prospects for the trust are good, the issue is fairly priced, and, of course, on whether you have the spare cash. A rights issue increases the supply of the company's shares on the market, and may therefore result in a temporary price reduction. If you do not wish to take up your rights you can sell your entitlement via your stockbroker or through the company.

b) Scrip issues (also called bonus, capitalisation or free issues)

A scrip issue is fundamentally a technical exercise. It gives each shareholder free of charge a number of new shares, depending on the number he holds. The idea is to translate capital shown in the balance sheet as accumulated capital reserves into issued share capital. No new money is raised, and the chief effect as far as the investor is concerned is to leave him with more shares at a lower price. You do not lose out. For example, you may start with 100 shares worth £2.50 each, and after the bonus issue you may end up with 500 shares worth 50p each. The value of your holding remains £250.

● 'B' shares

Investment trust 'B' shares are an anachronism which arose because of tax changes under past Finance Acts. They were designed to give an annual return in the form of additional shares rather than as dividend income, the idea being to reduce the income tax liability of shareholders who were higher rate taxpayers. 'B' shareholders receive no dividend, but are entitled to an annual scrip issue of fully-paid shares. The size of each year's scrip issue reflects the amount of dividend paid on the ordinary shares. 'B' shares can be converted at specified intervals into ordinary shares, and many have now disappeared through this method. Since 1975 there has been no tax advantage to UK investors in this arrangement, the annual scrip issue being treated as income and subject to tax.

● Preference shares

The preference shareholders come before the ordinary shareholders in the repayment queue on winding up, so to that extent their investment is safer than an ordinary shareholding. They also get a fixed dividend rate, which is normally cumulative. This means that if the company has to pass a preference dividend one year the arrears must be paid in a subsequent year, when they will take precedence over the dividends of ordinary shareholders.

Preference shareholders therefore enjoy a reasonably secure income, though it has no prospect for increasing. Their voting rights are usually restricted, so that they can only vote if the preference dividend is in arrears.

These shares were originally popular because they were seen as safer than ordinary shares, but after a period of high inflation and prolonged rising markets preference shares are no longer considered so attractive. The dividend, which would, when they were issued, have been pitched quite high, may after a few years seem very low. It may even have been outstripped by rising dividends on ordinary shares.

Preference shares are often thought of as fixed interest securities, though they are part of a trust's share capital. Dividends are fixed, so, like fixed interest securities, the market price will respond to changes in interest rates. However, most preference shares do not have a date at which the original capital is repaid, so there is not the same security as with a gilt, when you know in advance the date on which your capital will be repaid. In other words, preference shares have quite a lot of risk without very great rewards. The main holders of investment trust preference shares nowadays are the institutions, who need the relatively safe income to match their liabilities.

Loan capital

● Debenture stocks and loan stocks

Loan stocks are the traditional means by which investment trusts can boost the funds they invest on behalf of shareholders. They have been affected by rising interest rates and, like preference shares, have become much less common. Their original attraction was that they provided a high fixed return and considerable security since they took precedence over ordinary and preference shareholders in the event of a company being wound up. The loan stock holders, like any group of company creditors, can appoint a receiver if the trust defaults on its interest repayments.

There are two main classes of capital in this category: debenture stock and unsecured loan stock. They are both issued for a fixed term, at the end of which the original loan is repaid. The name of the stock, as with a gilt, carries the interest rate and the redemption date. For example, 12% Debenture 2013 will be repaid in the year 2013 and will pay a gross rate of interest of 12% each year. A title like 10.1% Redeemable Debenture Stock 1997/2002 means that the stock can be redeemed at any time between those two dates at the discretion of the investment trust's board. The AITC Year

Book gives repayment details on stocks in issue. '14 July 2004 at 105%' means that the stock will be repaid at that date with a 5% premium on the original capital. '1 May 1987 at par' means the stock was repaid at that date at the original face value.

There are certain differences between debenture stocks and unsecured loan stocks. Debentures are secured on the assets of the company, and among the classes of capital we are looking at they are highest in the ranking in the event that the trust is wound up. An unsecured loan stock, as the name suggests, has no asset security, and ranks after debenture stockholders but before preference and ordinary shareholders in the creditors' queue. Yields on unsecured loan stock are normally higher than for comparable debentures to reflect the greater level of risk.

Due to much higher interest rates in the last few years, companies have found it hard to issue loan stocks at competitive rates. One way round this has been the invention of 'STUDS', or stepped up interest debentures. These were introduced in the early eighties to provide trusts with the equivalent of a 'low start loan'. The rate of interest starts relatively low and rises over the life of the stock. For example, it might start at 6% and rise in annual steps of 1% to 14%. This means the interest load can be absorbed gradually, as the trust's income grows.

Borrowing by the whole industry, with total assets at 31 December 1986 of £20,494.5m and shareholders' funds at the same date of £19,014.5m was only £1,480m, or 7% of total assets. Of this, about £800m only was made up of long-term debt, the rest being currency loans or short-term debentures.

● Convertibles

A convertible is a loan stock or, less usually, a preference share, which carries the right to be converted into ordinary shares during a predetermined period of time. Most convertibles are unsecured loan stock (CULS) rather than debentures. Convertible debentures have the same advantage over CULS as their non-convertible equivalents in that they are secured against the company's assets.

Like other loan stocks, convertibles pay a fixed rate of

interest and have a fixed redemption date. As with a gilt, the price may rise or fall during the life of the stock but tends to move closer and closer to the face or par value as the redemption date approaches, unless there is some doubt about the financial soundness of the company.

As CULS offer a route into the ordinary shares they can be offered at a lower rate of interest than ordinary unsecured loan stock. In the early years their yield tends to be higher than on ordinary shares and because of their relationship with the company's equity capital the price will mirror changes in the ordinary share price.

Although there is a revival of interest generally in convertibles among institutional fund managers, there have not been many recent new issues of convertibles from investment trusts themselves, and it is far from easy to deal in investment trust convertibles.

● Prior charges

The expression 'prior charges' is an important piece of jargon in the investment trust industry. It refers to all types of stock, like debentures, unsecured loan stock, or preference shares, which rank ahead of ordinary shares when it comes to dividing up the trust's assets in the event of a winding up. In other words, they have a prior claim on the assets, and are described as a prior charge in the same way as your mortgage is a charge on your house – in other words, the building society has first claim on the sale proceeds.

There are two ways of valuing prior charges: at their par value ('prior charges at par') or at their market value ('prior charges at market'). The par value on, say, a debenture is the face value which is repaid at redemption. In other words, it is the agreed amount the company will pay to redeem the debenture if it is held to term. During its lifetime, the market value of the debenture will fluctuate. If there is still a long time until redemption, the value is usually less than par. The market will not value a prior charge very highly, because in most cases the interest rates paid on them are below current rates. Valuation 'at market' therefore takes the market price at a specified date and uses that to arrive at a value.

In order to work out how much of the trust's assets will be available for the ordinary shareholder, you need to know the value of any prior charges. How these are calculated will obviously make a difference. Calculating prior charges at par is the more conservative way of doing it. However, prior charges will only be deducted at par when they are repaid, or if the assets are realised and their value distributed to shareholders, as would happen in the event of a takeover, winding up or unitisation.

Prior charges may also be redeemed early, in which case they may be paid off at a premium to compensate investors for loss of a number of years interest. Investors who are buying investment trust shares in the hope of the trust being taken over will most likely want to value prior charges at par when doing their calculations. If you expect the trust whose shares you are buying to have a long and prosperous future, and regard your holding as long term, then valuing prior charges at market is good enough for your needs. You do not have to worry in the immediate future about the full par value being set against the trust's assets, and the money raised through prior charges is working for your benefit. Valuing at market value is also the better method of comparing two investment trusts with different borrowing structures.

The basis on which asset value is calculated for purposes of the AITC monthly performance figures takes prior charges at par, and assumes that convertible issues have been converted and only warrants have not been exercised.

● Warrants

A warrant is a contract which gives its owner the right to buy shares at some time in the future at a price which is fixed from the outset, and which is called the exercise price. If the warrant is exercised, in other words, if you buy the shares, then you will receive newly created shares in the trust.

The warrant has no income and no redemption value if it is not exercised. There is a specified time period during which it can be exercised, and once this period is over, the warrant has no value. There is no obligation on the warrant holder to buy shares, and if the share price does not rise above the

78

exercise price during the life of the warrant he will have no incentive to do so.

Warrants have become very popular in the investment trust industry. They offer the company another way of raising cash and give adventurous investors another investment route. The price paid for each warrant will usually be low compared to the share price but the warrant gives access to the potential high growth prospects of the ordinary shares.

For example, an investor may pay 30p for a warrant, giving him the right to subscribe for ordinary shares at 100p. The 'effective' price on the shares is therefore 130p. If this is higher than the current share price, the warrant is said to be at a premium to the ordinary shares. In the case quoted, if the shares are at 110p, the premium is 20p (130p-110p), or 18%. Warrant issues usually rise very quickly to stand at a premium over the ordinary share price. As far as the investor is concerned, the lower the premium the better. If there is no premium – as with a new warrant issue, or where the ordinary share price is rising rapidly – the warrants may represent an attractive opportunity.

Premiums will vary a lot, and will tend to increase as the life expectancy of the warrant reduces, providing there is a rising market. The more the share price rises, as one might expect over time, the better the chance of a profit. Warrant prices, like convertibles, will reflect the trust's ordinary share price, though they can be slow in catching up with equity price movements, and when they do they may move more dramatically. As you can see, making money through warrants is often a question of watching like a hawk for the right price relationships and then acting quickly.

If the exercise price is more than the current share price, warrants are said to be 'out of the money' and on the face of it are not worth buying. Such warrants may nevertheless change hands at attractive prices because of investors' expectations of what may happen to the share price. If the exercise price is less than the current share price, the warrants are 'in the money', and will have an inherent value equal to the difference between the two prices.

To show how gearing can work through warrants, here are two examples, one real and one imaginary. Early in 1987 the share price of Hambros Investment Trust stood at 240p, and the trust's warrants were priced at 91p. The warrants give the right to buy shares at 177p, which is less than the share price, so the warrants are 'in the money'. If the share price were to double to 480p, the warrants' intrinsic value would be 480p-177p = 303p. If you paid 91p for the warrants, and converted them when the share price had risen to 480p you would have a profit of 212p, or 133%, although the share price had only risen by 100%.

With the imaginary Newcomer Trust, the share price is 75p and the warrants stand at 15p. The warrants give the right to buy shares at 100p. The exercise price is higher than the share price, so the warrants are 'out of the money'. If the share price trebles to 225p, the warrants' intrinsic value will be 225p-100p = 125p. If you take up your share option under the warrant, you will be sitting on a profit of 110p (225p-115p) per share, which represents a profit of more than 700%. The ordinary shareholder would have enjoyed a 200% profit over the same time.

For those seeking information on warrants, some warrant prices are listed in the *Financial Times*, and details of warrants are given each month in the AITC Monthly Information Service. This includes subscription terms, price, premium and final year of exercise.

As far as the ordinary shareholders are concerned, warrants may not be an entirely desirable feature in an investment trust, since they effectively represent an issue of new shares. They are basically a deferred rights issue and issued initially to the existing shareholders as rights. If a shareholder sells his warrants or fails to exercise them he will suffer a reduction in his percentage share of the equity capital held, although he may have had the benefits of the sale proceeds. The extent of this reduction, or dilution as it is often called, will depend upon the difference between the share price and the exercise price, and upon the number of warrants exercised.

WARRANTS

Warrants give the holder the right, but not the obligation, to purchase shares at a fixed price at some date in the future, as stated in the subscription terms below. They provide the opportunity to participate in the capital growth of a company in a geared way. Price movements in the ordinary shares, up or down, are magnified in the price of the warrants.

Warrants have no voting rights and do not receive dividends. They can be bought and sold at any time before the exercise date and their prices are quoted in the press in the normal way. If a warrant is not exercised it expires without value.

Figures correct as at 31 December 1990

Company	Final Year of Exercise	Subscription Term	Warrant price pence	Share price pence	Warrant premium %
Abtrust New Dawn 'A'	1995	1 Ordinary at 95.88p	21.00	73.00	60.1
Abtrust New Dawn 'B'	1995	1 Ordinary at 135p	14.00	73.00	104.1
Abtrust New European	2000	1 Ordinary at 100p	21.00	67.00	80.6
Abtrust New Thai	1996	1 Ordinary at 100p	18.00	48.00	145.8
Anglo Scandinavian	1997	1 Ordinary at 100p	16.00	67.50	71.9
Baillie Gifford Shin Nippon	1996	1 Ordinary at 50p	66.00	93.50	24.1
Baillie Gifford Technology	1995	1 Ordinary at 45p	4.50	34.50	43.5
Beta Global Emerging	1996	1 Ordinary at 100p	13.00	58.00	94.8
CST Emerging Asia	1995	1 Ordinary at 50p	15.50	37.00	77.0
Castle Cairn	1999	1 Ordinary at 50p	11.00	31.50	93.7
Clydesdale	1995	1 Ordinary at 120p	13.00	66.50	100.0
Consolidated Venture Series "120"	1993	1 Ordinary at 120p	70.00	153.50	23.8
Continental Assets	1996	1 Ordinary at 100p	84.00	143.00	28.7
Drayton Asia	1995	1 Ordinary at 100p	18.00	55.50	112.6

81

Company	Final Year of Exercise	Subscription Term	Warrant price pence	Share price pence	Warrant premium %
Drayton English & International	1993	4 Ordinary at 70p	145.00	96.00	10.7
Drayton Far Eastern	1991	4 Ordinary at 25.25p	228.00	82.50	−0.3
ECU Trust	1997	1 Ordinary at 50p	12.00	41.50	49.4
EFM Dragon	1996	1 Ordinary at 10p	4.00	8.50	64.7
EFM Dragon Warrants 2005	2005	1 Ordinary at 15p	5.00	8.50	135.3
EFM Java	2000	1 Ordinary at 50p	15.00	34.00	91.2
European Project	1996	1 Ordinary at 50p	11.50	33.50	83.6
F & C Enterprise	1991	1 Ordinary at 20p	9.50	30.50	−3.3
F & C Enterprise Services "B"	1991	1 Ordinary at 31p	2.00	30.50	8.2
F & C Germany	2000	1 Ordinary at 135.63p	33.00	98.00	72.1
F & C Pacific	1994	1 Ordinary at 77.5p	79.00	135.00	15.9
First Ireland	1996	1 Ordinary at 100p	10.00	54.00	103.7
First Philippine	1996	1 Ordinary at 50p	7.00	24.00	137.5
First Spanish	1997	1 Ordinary at 100p	24.50	62.50	99.2
Fleming European Fledgeling	1997	1 Ordinary at 100p	23.00	64.50	90.7
Fleming High Income	1996	1 Ordinary at 100p	15.00	89.50	28.5
GT Venture	1993	1 Ordinary at 100p	9.50	68.50	59.9
Gartmore Emerging Pacific	1997	1 Ordinary at 64p	28.00	37.00	148.6
Gartmore European	1996	4 Ordinary at 88.5p	108.00	80.50	43.5
German	1999	1 Ordinary at 100p	19.50	77.50	54.2
German Smaller Companies	1995	1 Ordinary at 100p	100.00	188.00	6.4
Glasgow Income	1994	1 Ordinary at 55p	3.00	38.50	50.6
Greece Fund	1993	20 Ordinary at $10	17210.37	1284.36	7.3

Company	Final Year of Exercise	Subscription Term	Warrant price pence	Share price pence	Warrant premium %
Greenfriar	1995	1 Ordinary at 334p	43.00	241.00	56.4
Henderson Highland	1999	1 Ordinary at 100p	20.00	84.50	42.0
Independent Investment	1997	1 Ordinary at 79p	9.50	29.50	200.0
Jersey Phoenix	1996	1 Ordinary at 100p	13.50	75.00	51.3
Korea Liberalisation	1996	1 Ordinary at $10.50	156.00	306.00	128.8
Latin American	2005	1 Ordinary at $1	16.19	32.38	110.0
Leveraged Opportunity	1996	1 Ordinary at 100p	18.00	38.00	210.5
London American Ventures	1990	1 Ordinary at 110p	13.00	31.50	290.5
Martin Currie European	1998	1 Ordinary at 100p	21.00	73.00	65.8
Martin Currie Pacific	1993	1 Ordinary at 100p	123.00	205.00	8.8
Mediterranean Fund	1995	1 Ordinary at $95	21.50	4450.00	11.1
Merlin International Green	2000	1 Ordinary at 100p	18.00	73.00	61.6
Moorgate	1997	1 Ordinary at 128.5p	23.00	94.50	60.3
Multitrust	1991	1 Ordinary at 60p	3.50	35.00	81.4
New Throgmorton (1983)	1993	1 Capital at 50p	25.00	55.00	36.4
North American Gas	1995	1 Ordinary at 100p	20.00	66.00	81.8
Overseas	1998	1 Ordinary at 202p	83.00	189.00	50.8
Pacific Assets	1995	1 Ordinary at 100p	85.00	140.00	32.1
Pacific Horizon	1995	1 Ordinary at 50p	7.00	23.00	147.8
Pacific Property	1995	1 Ordinary at 50p	10.50	29.50	105.1
River & Mercantile	2000	1 Capital at 300p	28.00	86.00	281.4
River & Mercantile American	1999	1 Capital at 32.5p	9.50	16.50	154.5
River & Mercantile Extra Income	2000	1 Ordinary at 100p	14.50	90.50	26.5

Company	Final Year of Exercise	Subscription Term	Warrant price pence	Share price pence	Warrant premium %
River & Mercantile Smaller Co's	1996	1 Ordinary at 100p	18.00	84.50	39.6
River Plate	1996	1 Capital at 250p	15.50	58.00	357.8
Scottish Investment	1995	1 Ordinary at 161.33p	29.50	140.50	35.8
Scottish National	1998	1 Capital at 300p	9.00	45.00	586.7
Shires	1993	1 Ordinary at 182p	34.00	200.50	7.7
Siam Selective	1993	1 Ordinary at 100p	22.00	81.00	50.6
Smaller Companies	1998	1 Ordinary at 100p	16.00	68.00	70.6
Sphere	1995	1 Ordinary at 50p	7.50	23.50	144.7
Strata	1993	1 Ordinary at 100p	28.00	111.00	15.3
TR European Growth**	1997	1 Ordinary at 100p	40.00	87.00	60.9
TR Far East Income	1996	1 Ordinary at 105p	13.00	61.00	93.4
TR High Income*	1996	1 Ordinary at 100p	25.00	86.00	45.3
Thornton Asian	1995	1 Ordinary at 100p	17.00	66.00	77.3
Thornton Pan European	1993	1 Ordinary at 40p	7.50	26.00	82.7
Throgmorton Trust	1993	1 Ordinary at 39p	24.00	59.00	6.8
Throgmorton USM	1993	1 Ordinary at 100p	20.00	93.50	28.3
Trust of Property Shares	2000	1 Ordinary at 110p	11.00	47.00	157.4
Turkey Trust	2000	1 Ordinary at 207.87p	40.00	143.00	73.3
Value & Income 89/94	1994	1 Ordinary at 70p	10.00	55.50	44.1
Witan	1993	1 Ordinary at 76.5p	64.00	132.00	6.4

*Subscription Shares, which pay a fixed annual dividend of 1.5p each year
**Participating Subscription Shares, which pay the same dividend as that declared for the ordinary Shareholders.

CHAPTER EIGHT:
SPLIT-CAPITAL TRUSTS

A few trusts are set up from the outset as limited life trusts. That means it is agreed that the trust will be wound up and the assets distributed to shareholders at some fixed point in the future. Trusts like this are either wound up on specific date or shareholders must have the option to vote on a winding up between certain dates. The articles of association will give all the details.

The purpose of having a limited life trust is to control the discount, the difference between the share price and assets per share. As the trust moves towards its winding-up date the discount will inevitably narrow because when the trust is wound up shareholders receive the value of the trust's assets minus realisation costs. The limited life arrangement gives investors a measure of protection, and means they will not have to take it into their own hands to instigate change if discounts widen.

A limited life trust does impose certain investment constraints on the fund managers. As the life of the trust is either relatively short or of uncertain duration, it is hard for managers to set up new borowing or to invest in assets, like unquoted stocks, which are difficult to sell in the short term. However, there is one class of trust which always has a limited life: split capital trusts.

Twin objectives

The traditional return for investors in investment trusts consists of a combination of capital and income. In response to modern tax changes which have introduced very high income tax levels, a new type of trust was invented in the

1960s. The idea of split capital trusts is to separate out the two types of return so that you can choose which suits you best. There are two types of share in split capital trusts: income and capital. The income shares get all the income and usually have a fixed redemption price. The capital shares receive all or most of the capital return. Split capital trusts have a limited life. Usually two dates are given, between which the trust must be wound up.

In this way, the capital investor knows when he is going to get his money back, and both types of investor can estimate the return they will get over the period between purchase and redemption, subject of course to assumptions about the level of capital and income growth. Income shares will appeal to investors who want a high and growing income and are not too concerned about capital growth. For example, a retired investor who is not a higher rate taxpayer and for whom income tax is only chargeable at the basic rate.

Capital shares will appeal to the opposite category of investor: those who do not need income at present and want to avoid paying additional income tax. This might be the case with a highly paid and therefore highly taxed person who wants to put away savings long term. It might equally be appropriate for money set aside for a child, where the shares need not be touched until the child is eighteen, and no income is needed in the meantime.

Split capital trusts which have been running for a long time have done well for investors, partly because they have a built-in gearing structure. Each class of shareholder benefits from this arrangement. The income shareholders' funds are generating an additional amount of capital gain for the capital shareholders, while the capital shareholders' funds are generating income for the income shareholders.

Time factor

Due to the limited life of a split capital trust, the amount of time left before winding up becomes a factor in the trust's share price and discount movements. An increasing income for years ahead is seen as very attractive, so income shares tend to stand at a premium to their redemption price. They will rise in price in the early years, as the income rises, and fall as the redemption date approaches, when the stream of income will come to an end.

Capital shares will stand at a high discount in the trust's early years because it will be a long time before shareholders can get their money back. This is in contrast to conventional trusts, where high discounts are usually related to poor performance or an unfashionable policy. It is possible to find young split capital trusts with a good performance record which are still on a very attractive discount.

Some people dislike the income shares of split capital trusts because they trade at a premium to their redemption value. That is, when the trust is wound up, the income shareholder makes a capital loss, though he has had the income in the meantime.

To get round this problem, a modified version of the split capital trust has appeared. With these trusts, the capital return is split in a fixed proportion between the income and capital shareholders. For example, the capital shareholders may get 75% and the income shareholders 25% of the assets. Such arrangements are designed to alleviate the capital loss on redemption from the income shares. However, as a quid pro quo for giving up part of their capital gain, the capital shareholders usually receive a share of the annual income.

Example

The example of an imaginary trust given on page 83 shows a traditional split capital trust, where the income shares get all the income but none of the capital growth, and the capital shares get all the capital growth but no income. The example assumes that there are 25m income shares and 25m capital shares in issue. Management expenses are 0.4% of the net asset value, and net asset value grows by 10% a year. The portfolio yield is 6%, and the company will be wound up after thirteen years in 2000. It is also assumed that the income shares were issued at 110p per share and the capital shares at 90p.

On the basis of the figures in the example, this would be a gross redemption yield, that is, an annualised return taking

87

Table: Split Capital Trust

Year	Net Assets £	Income shares net asset value p	Capital shares net asset value p	Total Gross Revenue	Capital Shares Earnings Gross pps	Income Shares Earnings pps*
1987	50,000,000	100.00	100.00	3,000,000	0.00	7.72
1988	55,000,000	100.00	120.00	3,300,000	0.00	8.49
1989	60,500,000	100.00	142.00	3,630,000	0.00	9.34
1990	66,550,000	100.00	166.20	3,993,000	0.00	10.28
1991	73,205,000	100.00	192.82	4,392,300	0.00	11.30
1992	80,525,500	100.00	222.10	4,831,530	0.00	12.43
1993	88,578,050	100.00	254.31	5,314,683	0.00	13.68
1994	97,435,855	100.00	289.74	5,846,151	0.00	15.04
1995	107,179,441	100.00	328.72	6,430,766	0.00	16.55
1996	117,897,385	100.00	371.59	7,073,643	0.00	18.20
1997	129,687,123	100.00	418.75	7,781,227	0.00	20.02
1998	142,655,835	100.00	470.62	8,559,350	0.00	22.03
1999	156,921,419	100.00	527.69	9,415,285	0.00	24.23
2000	172,613,561	100.00	590.45	10,356,814	0.00	26.65

Note: Figures supplied by Alexanders, Laing & Cruickshank.

* Net of tax and expenses

into account the proceeds at redemption, of 15.24% for the income shares and 15.56% for the capital shares.

In this example, the rate of increase in value each year of the capital shares gradually reduces, from 20% in year 2 to 12% in year 20. This is because the amount of increase is a smaller percentage of the assets at each date.

By contrast, the annual increase in earnings on the ordinary shares remains constant at 10%.

It goes without saying that split capital trusts are more complicated than ordinary investment trusts, and their capital structures vary quite a bit from one to another. Details of split capital structures and repayment terms are given in the AITC Year Book.

Investment tool

These trusts can be very attractive investment tools, but it is as well to get advice before you take the plunge. An adviser should be able to show you how to maximise the investment potential of such trusts. For instance, with a standard split capital trust where there is no capital appreciation for the income shares, which will therefore suffer a loss at redemption, it is possible to buy holdings in both income and capital shares so that the capital loss on the one would cancel out the gain on the other. This would effectively nullify any capital gains tax liability while producing the best of both worlds in terms of return.

At 31 December 1990 there were sixteen trusts in the split level category, and their average performance was generally above the UK capital growth sector average except in the very long term.

Split level trusts: performance results of £100 invested

	1 yr	5 yrs	10 yrs
Split level trusts*	92.8	209.0	531.6
UK Capital Growth	85.1	175.4	648.0
FT All Share	89.0	176.7	493.6

* Capital shares average performance.
All figures to 31.12.90. Source: AITC.

CHAPTER NINE:
CLINCHING THE BARGAIN

Buying and selling investment trust company shares is really very simple. You can place your order via a stockbroker, your bank or a suitably authorised financial adviser. The directory of independent financial advisers on page 157 will help you find an appropriate person to suit your needs. It has been compiled by the AITC based on information provided by the firms themselves.

To obtain the full benefit from any adviser it is important at the outset to define exactly what type of service you require.

● Discretionary

You give the broker the authority to deal on your behalf, without consulting you. He will, of course, let you know when he makes changes to your portfolio, and give you regular reports on how your investments are performing.

● Advisory

The broker gives you advice on which investments to choose, but you make the buying and selling decisions yourself.

● Dealing (executionary)

The broker simply does the buying and selling on your instructions, and will not offer advice.

Before selecting an adviser you should check the type of facilities each firm provides along with the cost and any minimum investment criterion. It is best to approach two or three advisers at the outset to give yourself some idea of comparative service and cost.

Since Big Bang, which abolished the minimum commission charges brokers were entitled to levy, charges on the different levels of service vary a lot. For all levels of service there will be a commission charge on purchases and sales, and for discretionary and advisory services there may also be an annual management charge. Some brokers encourage investors to use their discretionary service by imposing a lower minimum investment, or lower charges. Others take the reverse view, on the grounds that discretionary is the more 'de luxe' service, and design their advisory service as the more accessible of the two.

Placing your order

If you are not familiar with buying and selling shares the whole idea of contacting a stockbroker and arranging the transaction may seem rather off-putting. In fact, the process is just as simple as phoning up and ordering cinema tickets with your credit card. Indeed one London stockbroker has even introduced its very own credit card for sharebuyers to help reduce the formality which people associate with the process of buying shares.

So what happens when you approach a stockbroker with your first order? Do not be put off if the broker asks for some details about your financial affairs. Most shares are usually bought on credit so the stockbroker is taking the same sort of care as the credit card company would before issuing you with a plastic card. The normal procedure is to give your bank as a reference. It may take a few days for the reference to be taken up but providing the broker receives the green light, you are ready to go.

1. Place your order

Remember to specify clearly the number of shares you require and, if you wish, the price range you are prepared to deal at. Most brokers will check their computer terminals for the price of the share but as prices dart around minute by minute there may be some small fluctuation.

91

2. Bargains reported

All share deals are known as 'bargains', although in this sense the term does not indicate that you have bought something on the cheap. Your broker will telephone you with the confirmed details of your purchase once the bargain has been struck.

3. Contract note dispatched

The contract note is similar to a store receipt. It will tell you how many shares have been purchased, at what price and on what date. It will indicate the date when you have to pay for the shares. This is known as the settlement date.

4. Pay for shares

Most people pay for their shares by simply sending a cheque for the appropriate amount to their stockbroker, making sure it arrives by the stated settlement date. Some companies may run deposit accounts in tandem with their share dealing service in which case it may be possible to arrange for funds to be transferred directly.

5. Receive the share certificate

A few weeks after you buy the shares you will receive your share certificate. This is sent to you by the company whose shares you have purchased. So if there is any delay contact the company direct, not your broker. Keep this safe as it is proof of your ownership.

When you decide to sell your shares, you reverse the process. Contact your broker and give him your instructions. You will be sent a transfer form once the bargain has been completed, together with your contract note. You sign this and return it with your share certificate.

CHAPTER TEN:
PACKAGED DEALS

There are several types of packaged deals available for those keen to buy investment trust company shares. These are available through investment trust managers in some cases or from investment dealing companies who specialise in share-based investment products.

Regular savings plans

A very attractive way to buy investment trust shares for the small investor is a regular savings plan. These have only become widely available in the last six or seven years, and are now offered by a number of groups. With a regular savings plan, as the name suggests, you do not need to buy a block of shares worth hundreds or even thousands of pounds. You can invest as little as £20 a month. There are now twenty-six groups offering regular savings schemes. Table One prepared by the AITC gives the basic features of each scheme, but you should obtain full details direct from the company concerned if you are considering an investment.

Though these schemes are known as regular savings plans, in practice most can be used for three different purposes: regular savings, occasional savings of a lump sum, and reinvestment of dividends. If you want to save regularly you set up a monthly standing order with your bank to pay a sum into the trust you have chosen. The minimum may be as low as £20 a month, and the highest minimum quoted is £50. The minimum monthly investment usually applies to each separate trust you want to buy shares in.

The trust managers amalgamate the orders from the regular savings scheme investors, and buy shares in a block once a

*I*nvestment *T*rust *S*avings

Manager	Regular Savings Min Monthly	Lump Sum Min	Dividend Reinvestment	Purchase	Selling Facility
ALLIANCE AND SECOND ALLIANCE TRUST (SELF MANAGED)	£25	£250	Yes	Monthly: money received by 5th	Yes
ARGOSY ASSET MANAGEMENT plc	£50	£2,000*	Yes	Monthly: money received by 20th day Lump sums: weekly	Yes
BAILLIE GIFFORD & CO	£30	£250*	Yes	Lump sums over £5000 daily Lump sums £250 – £5000 weekly Monthly: money received by 20th	Yes
BARING PRIVATE INVESTMENT MANAGEMENT LIMITED	£25	£250	Yes	Money cleared by 20th	Yes
DUNEDIN FUND MANAGERS LTD	£30	£250	Yes	Monthly: money received by 15th Lump sums: twice weekly	Yes
EDINBURGH FUND MANAGERS	£30	£250	Yes	Monthly: money received by 20th Lump sums weekly	Yes
FLEMING INVESTMENT TRUST MANAGEMENT LTD	£25****	£250***	Yes	Lump sums over £5,000 daily under £5,000 weekly	Yes: lump sums over £5,000 daily under £5,000 weekly
FOREIGN & COLONIAL MANAGEMENT LTD	£25	£250	Yes	Twice monthly: money received by 14th or 28th	Yes
GT MANAGEMENT PLC	£25	£500	Yes	Monthly: money cleared by 15th	Yes: monthly
GARTMORE INVESTMENT & GARTMORE SCOTLAND	£20	£250	Yes	Monthly: money cleared by 20th Lump sums £250-£1,000: monthly Over £ 1,000: asap	Yes
GLASGOW INVESTMENT MANAGERS LTD	£20	£200	Yes	Monthly: money received by 10th Lump sums within 10 days	Yes
JOHN GOVETT & CO LTD	£25	£250***	Yes	Monthly: money cleared by 20th	Yes: monthly

and *I*nvestment *S*chemes

Commission	Other Charges †	Other Features/Schemes
Subject to competitive tender	Purchase 50p sale £5	PEP scheme available
Nil	Arrangement fee: 3% Admin Charge: 0.25% No charge for sales. Investors can choose to pay up to 3% to intermediaries, if used, on lump sum investments, in which case the arrangement fee is waived by Argosy.	Free telephone dealing facility for financial advisers.
Nil	Sale £10	Dividends & interest from any other investments may be used to buy shares.
0.5% Purchase: min £1 Sale: min £10	Nil	
Nil	Nil	Regular statements Non-certificated plan 'Savings for Children' option PEP scheme available.
0.2% purchase 1.5% sale Under £7,000 0.5% sale, over £7,000 min £25	Sale or transfer £10	
Nil, but see other charges	Purchase 1% min £1 max £50 Sale 1% min £10 Investors can choose to pay up to 3% on lump sum investments to intermediaries, if used.	A non-certificated plan Share "exchange" facility PEP scheme available.
0.2% purchase/sale	Nil	Dividends and interest from any UK company may be used to buy shares. Mortgage facility available.
Expected to be nil, or at low institutional rates of commission	Investors will bear a proportionate share of the total cost of acquiring or disposing of shares (including any stamp duty) and, if applicable, any brokers' commission.	
Nil, in exceptional cases not exceeding 0.2%	Nil	Share "exchange" facility Scheme covers all classes of share capital.
0.2% purchase 0.2% sale, min £10	Purchase: nil Sale: £10 admin charge per transaction	
Purchase nil Sale 0.25%	1% purchase min £1 1% sale min £10	Share "exchange" facility Gift facility

Source: AITC (December 1990)

95

Manager	Regular Savings Min Monthly	Lump Sum Min	Dividend Reinvestment	Purchase	Selling Facility
GUINNESS MAHON FUND MANAGERS LTD	£25	£250	Yes	Monthly and lump sums under £1,000: money cleared by 15th Lump sums over £1,000 on Wednesday after money cleared	Yes: available twice in any 12 months
HAMBROS BANK LTD	£30	£300	Yes	Monthly: money received by 25th	No special arrangement
HENDERSON ADMINISTRATION LTD	£50	£250	Yes⬚	Monthly: money cleared by 15th Weekly: lump sums	Yes: if shares held for 6 months, available twice in any 12 months
IVORY & SIME PLC	£20		Yes	Monthly: money received by 13th	Yes: no charge
		£2,000	No	Daily	Yes: no charge
KLEINWORT BENSON INVESTMENT MANAGEMENT LTD	£25	£250	Yes	Monthly: money received by end of month Lump sums over £10,000 asap	Yes: monthly
MIM LTD	£25	£1,000	Yes	Monthly: money cleared by 15th Lump sums: daily	Yes
MARTIN CURRIE INVESTMENT MANAGEMENT LTD	£20**	£200	Yes	Monthly: money cleared by 5th Weekly: lump sums received by Friday Daily: lump sums over £10,000	Will be executed on instruction from holder
MERCURY ASSET MANAGEMENT PLC	£50	£500	Yes	Monthly: money received by 20th	Yes: weekly
MORGAN GRENFELL TRUST MANAGERS LTD	£30	£250	Yes	Monthly: money received by 15th	Yes: if shares held for 6 months
MURRAY JOHNSTONE LTD	£30	£250	Yes⬚	Monthly: money received by 7th day Lump sums: daily	Yes
SCOTTISH INVESTMENT TRUST (SELF MANAGED)	£25	£250	Yes	Twice monthly: on second and final Fridays Daily: lump sums over £10,000	Yes: if shares held for 6 months
STEWART IVORY & CO LTD	£25	£250	Yes	Twice monthly: money cleared by a) first Monday b) third Monday	Yes: if shares held for 6 months, available twice in any 12 months
THROGMORTON INVESTMENT MANAGEMENT LTD	£25	£250	Yes	Monthly: money received by 6th day of each month	Yes: if shares held for 6 months
TOUCHE, REMNANT & CO	£25	£250	Yes	Monthly: money received by 15th Weekly: lump sums under £5,000 Daily: lump sums over £5,000	Yes

† Charges shown do not include stamp duty or VAT *£100 min subsequent contributions **may be paid quarterly ***£25 min subsequent contributions ****may be paid annually, half-yearly, quar
This table is intended only as a guide to the savings and investment schemes which are available, full details of the individual schemes should be obtained before entering into any transactio

Commission	Other Charges †	Other Features/Schemes
Not exceeding 0.2%	Nil	PEP scheme available
See other charges	A proportionate share of total cost	
Nil but see other charges Sale: 1.5% min £10	Purchase: 1.5% min £2.50 max £25	Statements issued quarterly Gift facility PEP scheme available
Nil Nil but see other charges	Nil 0.25% admin charge 3% arrangement fee	Lump sum facility available after 12 months' regular saving Telephone dealing service with full back up facilities available for financial advisers PEP scheme available
Nil but see other charges	Purchase 0.5% min £1 Sale 1% min £10	PEP scheme available
Monthly savers: 0.2% purchase, 0.2% sale min £10. Lump sum investors: 1% purchase max £50, 1% sale min £10	3% commission paid to intermediaries on lump sums £2.50 transfer stamp duty from nominee company	
Nil but see other charges	3% commission paid to intermediaries on lump sums Sale: £5.75	Dividends and interest from any UK company may be used to buy shares
Nil	Sale: 1.5% Share certificate: £10	Biannual statements 'Savings for Children'
0.2%	Sale: minimum commission per sale on behalf of one or more investors is £10, to be shared between them, plus fixed handling charge of £10 each	Dividends and interest from any other investments may be used to buy shares
0.2% purchase/sale	3% commission paid to intermediaries on lump sums	PEP scheme available
Nil	Sale: £10	Gift Plan Trustee Plan – for charities and non-profit- making organisations
0.2% purchase/sale	Sale: £10	Consolidated share certificate issued every 6 months. Dividends from other investments may be used to buy shares PEP scheme available
Nil purchase/sale	50p transfer stamp duty from nominee company	Dividends and interest from other stocks and shares may be used to buy shares. Statements issued twice a year
1% purchase/sale	£5 transfer into and out of scheme 3% commission paid to intermediaries on lump sums	Share "exchange" facility Statements issued twice a year Switch facility PEP scheme available Dividends and interest from other stocks and shares may be used to buy shares

▫ Available for regular savers only

Source: AITC (December 1990)

month. As a result, there are considerable economies of scale, which means the charges on the regular savings purchase will be less than if you bought such a small number of shares yourself. You might find, for instance, that a stockbroker charged a minimum commission of £25 on each transaction. However as the groups concerned are large institutional investors, they can take negotiate very low commission rates on share dealings and most will pass this benefit on to the investor.

Unlike unit trusts, where fractions of a unit can be bought, it is not possible to buy less than a whole share. With regular contributions of, say, £20 a month, the amount saved is unlikely to correspond to an exact number of shares. To get round this problem, the managers will keep the small leftover amounts in cash, and will add them to later contributions to buy shares in subsequent months.

You are not committed to an investment trust regular savings scheme in the same way as to a regular premium insurance policy. You can stop contributions usually without restriction, except that you might have to give one month's notice. With schemes where more than one trust is available, you can also usually switch your future contributions into another trust of your choice.

When it comes to selling your shares it will depend upon which you have chosen. In some schemes the managers will make the disposal for you. In others, the sale has to be made through a stockbroker. Shares in regular savings schemes are often held in nominee accounts – that is, they are held in a separate account, without being allotted to each of the individual shareholders by name. This does not, of course, put your title to the shares in any doubt, but it means that the paperwork is reduced considerably and you do not eventually finish up with masses of share certificates, each for a few shares. If you leave the scheme you will have the shares transferred into your own name.

Additional features

Apart from their regular savings aspect, these schemes also offer the possibility of making one-off lump sum purchases of trust shares. The minimum varies greatly depending on which scheme you choose as the table shows, ranging from £250 to £2,000.

You can use the occasional savings facility to add to your own savings, to make savings on an irregular basis without having a regular savings plan, or to buy shares as a gift for someone else.

Finally, most regular savings plans can be used for the reinvestment of dividends. Although total return figures quoted for investment trusts notionally reinvest dividends in order to reflect the income aspect of the return, it was not possible for the investor to reinvest his dividends automatically until regular savings plans became common.

The dividends reinvested can be from the trust in which shares are being bought through the regular savings aspect of the scheme, from another trust in which the saver holds shares, or even, with some schemes, from any other company – investment trust or otherwise – of which the investor is a shareholder. In this case, all you have to do is instruct the registrar of the company concerned to pay your dividends direct to the investment trust savings scheme.

Personal Equity Plans

Personal Equity Plans (PEPs) were announced in the 1986 Budget, and the first plans went on sale on 1 January 1987. The PEP scheme is designed to encourage investors to buy UK quoted shares. The maximum investment per person for the tax year 1990/1, was £6,000 and the returns are tax free.

Since investment trusts are quoted by UK companies, it was a considerable disappointment for the industry that at the outset no more than 25% of the permitted investment could be in investment trusts.

However, persistent lobbying by the industry has improved matters considerably. You may now invest up to £3,000 in a so-called qualifying investment trust, which is a trust where at least 50% of the assets are invested in the UK. If you wish to invest in a non-qualifying trust the ceiling is a more miserly £900.

The AITC has produced a table giving the main features of

Investment Trust Personal Equity Plan

MANAGER	TRUSTS AVAILABLE		Initial	Annual
ALLIANCE TRUST SAVINGS LTD	Alliance Second Alliance		Nil	Nil
DUNEDIN FUND MANAGERS LTD	Dundee and London (p) Dunedin Income Growth (p) Dunedin Worldwide Edinburgh		£24 set up	0.5% (c) 1.0% (e)
FLEMING INVESTMENT TRUST MANAGEMENT LTD	Fleming American Fleming Claverhouse (p) Fleming Enterprise (p) Fleming Far Eastern Fleming High Income (p)	Fleming Int High Income Fleming Japanese Fleming Mercantile (p) Fleming Overseas Fleming Universal	1.5% (c) (d) 1.5% (e)	£25 (a) (c) (d) 1.25% (e)
GARTMORE INVESTMENT LIMITED	Scottish National (p) (Income, Capital and Zero Dividend Shares only)		5%	1.5%
GLASGOW INVESTMENT MANAGERS	Glasgow Income Trust (p) Shires (p)		Details available from the managers	
GUINNESS MAHON FUND MANAGERS LTD	Temple Bar (p)		£50	1.0% (b)
HENDERSON FINANCIAL MANAGEMENT LTD	Henderson Highland (p) Lowland (p) Witan (p)		5.0%	1.5%
IVORY & SIME PLC	British Assets (p) First Charlotte (p) I & S Optimum Income (p) Investors Capital (p) Pacific Assets Personal Assets Selective Assets		£50	1.25%
KLEINWORT BENSON INVESTMENT MANAGEMENT LTD	Jos (p) Kleinwort Smaller Companies (p) Merchants (p)		3.5% (c) 5.0% (e)	1.0%
MIM LIMITED	English & International (p)		5%	1.25%
MOORGATE INVESTMENT MANAGEMENT LIMITED	General Consolidated (p) Moorgate (p)		2%	1.25%
MURRAY JOHNSTONE LTD	Murray Income (p) Murray International Murray Smaller Markets Murray Ventures		1.5%	1.25%
RIVER & MERCANTILE INVESTMENT MANAGEMENT LTD	River & Mercantile Trust (p) River & Mercantile Extra Income (p) River & Mercantile Smaller Companies (p)		3.75%	1.0%
STEWART IVORY & CO LTD	Scottish American (p)		3.0%	1.25%
TOUCHE REMNANT & CO	TR City of London (p)		Nil	1.0%

(a) per shareholding
† Charges shown do not include stamp duty or VAT.
(p) indicates the trust intends to comply with the 50% in the UK rule.
This table is intended only as a guide to the PEP schemes which are available. Full details of the individual schemes should be obtained before entering into any transactions.

(b) subject to a minimum of £35

(c) investment trust shares

(d) other UK shares (self select)

CHARGES[†] _Dealing_	TOP UP FACILITY AVAILABLE	MONTHLY PAYMENT FACILITY – MINIMUM
0.15%	YES	£50
Nil (c) 0.25% (e)	YES	£30
1.75% (c) (d) 1.50% (e)	YES	£100
Up to 0.75%	YES	£50
0.2% (c) 0.25% (e) 1.5% or £25 (d) whichever higher	YES	£100
0.25%	YES	£100
3.25% (f) initial 0.25% share switch	YES	£50
0.5%	YES	–
0.2% brokerage may be levied	YES	Nil
0.25%	YES	£100
0.3%	YES	£100
0.25% (e)	YES	£250
0.3%	YES	£150
1.0%	NO	£50

(e) other UK shares (managed portfolio)   _(f) 3% waived if financial advisers forego commission_

investment trust PEPs and you will see the letter (p) after a trust if it is a qualifying investment. The table gives you an idea of costs, top-up facilities and any facility for monthly investment. It was prepared in December 1990 and is intended as a guide only. You should obtain full details of the schemes which you are interested in before going ahead.

Life insurance products

Without actually buying the shares yourself, it is possible to invest indirectly in investment trusts through life insurance and pensions products. You can do this through single premium insurance bonds, regular premium insurance policies, and pensions plans. The point is to combine the tax and other advantages of the packaged product with the investment performance of the trust.

A regular premium policy will usually involve saving monthly for a term of ten years, after which all proceeds are free of tax. There is also a small amount of life insurance attached. Regular premium life policies are not as attractive nowadays as they used to be, since tax relief on premiums was abolished in 1984. The way in which the life fund is taxed and the charges levied on the policy also out them at a disadvantage to direct investment.

Single premium bonds are also attractive to many people, though their proceeds are not tax free as those of a regular premium policy are. Basic rate taxpayers will pay no extra tax on profits from a bond, but higher rate taxpayers will incur a liability if they withdraw more than 5% of the original investment from the bond annually, and when they finally cash in the investment. At this point, all the profits over the life of the bond are amalgamated and taxed at the investor's highest income tax rate, though the liability is reduced by top-slicing relief.

In short, bonds have a complicated tax treatment which makes them unattractive, particularly to the higher rate taxpayer. Due to tax considerations, buying trust shares direct is likely to give you a better after-tax return than investing through a bond, though the bond offers the advantage of automatic annual withdrawals.

Pension plans where the fund is invested in investment trust shares are rather different. Pension funds are free of all tax and there is full tax relief on your contributions up to statutory limits. For someone starting a regular premium plan the investment possibilities and the pound cost averaging effect make such plans very attractive. Pension planning is extremely complex and readers are advised to consult an independent financial adviser who specialises in this area of investment.

Unit trusts

Investment trusts are also regarded as an acceptable specialisation for the unit trust industry, and there is a separate Investment Trust Units sector which comprised ten unit trusts in the winter of 1990. The table below shows how this sector has performed compared to investment trusts as a whole.

Table: Performance of Investment Trust Units

	1 year	5 years	10 years
Sector top performer	−6.53	95.04	401.17
Sector average performer	−13.32	63.87	297.51
Sector bottom performer	−25.80	11.39	199.09
Investment trust sector average	−18.17	69.73	337.12

Source: Micropal
Figures show % growth offer to bid to 1.1.1991

Where performance is concerned, it seems that buying unit trusts which specialise in investment trust shares is usually less rewarding than buying investment trust shares direct. However, if you can pick the top performing unit trust in this sector it outperforms the average investment trust. As investment trusts represent a significant percentage of the total market UK capitalisation, managers of general trust units may well also hold investment trust shares.

These results are not very conclusive. Generally, it is important to obtain sound financial advice and to ensure that whether you choose to invest in shares through investment trusts, unit trusts, pension plans, personal equity plans or life assurance products that you buy the right product to suit your personal requirements. This should take into consideration many factors including your age, income, existing savings and insurance, tax bracket, timescale of investment and attitude to risk.

CHAPTER ELEVEN:
SOURCES OF INFORMATION

Keeping track of events in the money world and the progress of your particular investment be it shares, investment trusts or unit trusts will require quite a lot of time and effort, but it is well worth it. Even if you decide to delegate the actual buying and selling decisions to your stockbroker or investment adviser it is still a good idea to be as fully informed as possible about your own shareholdings.

Performance

The main source of information on the recent performance of investment trusts is the Monthly Information Service from the AITC. Figures are calculated to the end of the month, and the share price performance details are available in the month following.

MIS includes: share price total return, net asset value total return, and net asset value performance and total return combined. It also provides details of monthly savings schemes, personal equity plans and managers' addresses.

Share price total return and net asset total return figures are given over one, five, seven and ten years, on a 'result of £100 invested' basis. The MIS gives the top twenty performers over each period, the average performances for the categories, average discounts, and the results for each period of all the AITC member trusts, listed alphabetically, by category, or by management group.

The MIS is available on subscription from the AITC. The cost is £20 a year for the full service, which includes a quarterly newsletter.

Apart from the MIS, share price details for many trusts are

published daily, just as for any quoted share in the prices pages of a number of newspapers, notably the *Financial Times,* the *Daily Telegraph* and *The Times*. Apart from the previous day's price, useful figures given usually include the share price high and low for the previous year, and the gross yield. The *Financial Times* also publishes daily net asset values for investment trusts.

A good deal of useful information, and comprehensive performance analysis, are given in the quarterly publication *Investment Trusts* which is the only magazine devoted entirely to investment trusts. The *Investors Chronicle* also comments periodically on investment trusts, as well as publishing regular detailed surveys.

These are probably the chief sources of information which are easily accessible to private investors and are designed with their needs most in mind. The City pages of the newspapers also cover investment trusts, and report news such as bids, takeovers, unitisations and new issues.

Report and accounts

Probably the most important source for anyone considering investing in a company is its annual report and accounts. Reading the company's annual report and accounts is not quite such a technical business for an investment trust as it is for a conventional trading company, because an investment trust's operations are simpler by comparison. The report and accounts sum up the past year's performance and give an idea of the trust's progress over a number of years.

Investment trust managers are happy to send free copies of their report and accounts to interested parties on request. The industry has done a lot to make these documents as attractive, accessible and informative as possible. Investment trust managers give simple summaries of performance, clear analyses of recent changes, and plenty of information on the stocks in which the company has invested, all accompanied by tables and graphs which make the data much easier to follow.

A large number of questions can be answered from the information given in the report and accounts:

- what has performance been like during the year, and how does this compare to last year and earlier years?
- how did the portfolio change during the year?
- were there any new share issues during the year, or any changes in structure, such as increased gearing?
- who are the directors and managers of the trust?
- what is the dividend for the current year, and how does this compare to previous years?
- what sort of investment philosophy do the managers have?
- what does the portfolio of investments currently consist of? How concentrated is it? What types of company does it invest in? What reasons are given for the investments made? Which areas have done well, and which not so well? What changes are planned for the coming year?

Foreign and Colonial

In order to give some idea of what investment trust reports are like, we have taken the 1986 Foreign and Colonial report, the Revenue Account and Balance Sheet are on pages 105 and 109.

Foreign and Colonial, the oldest and possibly best known investment trust, produces particularly good information for its shareholders, with a welter of illustrations. For the year ended 31 December 1986 it has a very good story to tell, and the report begins, as is traditional, with a summary of results: net assets, net assets per share, net revenue, earnings per shares and dividends per share.

Summary of Results

Attributable to ordinary shareholders	1986	1985	
Net assets	£708.5m	£507.3m	+40%
Net assets per share (Prior charges at nominal value)	134.8p	96.5p	+40%
Net revenue	£9.0m	£7.9m	+14%
Earnings per share	1.72p	1.51p	+14%
Dividends per share	1.69p	1.47p	+15%

The Chairman's Statement goes into performance in more detail: the net asset value is up by 40% over the year, and the trust's share price by 56%. In fact, on a total performance basis, the trust was the seventeenth best performer in the industry.

The reasons for the trust's good performance are given as its high exposure to, and good performance in, the Japanese market; its substantial borrowings and their effective investment in a period of rising markets (what gearing's all about!), and the fact that most borrowings were in sterling and US dollars, both of which had periods of weakness, while half the assets were in the strong currency yen and deutschmark bloc markets.

The trust's revenue was up by 22%, due to increases in dividends from the companies in which the trust had invested, as well as record underwriting commission (see below). There is some explanation of increased expenses: management expenses are up but are partly offset by dividends received from the management company – a subsidiary in which the trust has a majority holding. Increased interest paid reflects higher borrowings. The final dividend recommended brings the total dividend for the year to 1.69p per share – up 15% on 1985.

The Chairman then comments on a number of individual topics with policy statements or reactions to events relevant to the trust's progress. Big Bang has, on the whole, proved favourable: 'It has been easier to buy and sell shares in size and we have been able to reduce commissions paid by about 30%.' The limitations on investment trust holdings in Personal Equty Plans have been 'disappointing', and have meant that PEPs have proved 'impossible to provide economically'.

The possibility of a Tokyo listing for Foreign and Colonial, hopefully to take place during 1987, is mentioned. As for future prospects, the board sees investment opportunities in a number of markets, but is cautious about the possibility of long-standing bull markets drawing to an end.

The directors and managers are listed. A short paragraph of biography is given for each director, and we find that the trust is jointly managed by two of the directors, backed up

107

by a team of six assistants.

A series of market reviews summarises what has happened in the main markets in which the trust has invested, and mentions the main companies which have done well in each. There are breakdowns of the portfolio by industrial and geographical classification, and views on currencies together with details of portfolio exposure to each.

At the end of 1986 Foreign and Colonial was 32.7% invested in the UK (compared to 34.8% in 1985), 23.6% in the US (compared to 29.1%), 18.0% in Japan (16.5%), 21.7% in Europe (15.7%) and 3.5% in the Far East excluding Japan (3.2%).

As a further measure of performance, a comparison is shown between the Foreign and Colonial share price performance over five years and the constituent companies of the *Financial Times* 30 Share Index. Foreign and Colonial's price rose by 252% over the period, compared to the index's 148%. The investment trust in terms of performance ranking, comes ninth among the index companies.

There follow details of how to buy shares through the trust's regular savings plan, and tables analysing the breakdown of ordinary shareholders (24.2% of them are individuals). A brief history of the company is followed by ten-year records of asset and revenue performance, showing growth in net asset value and dividends (an extract from the Revenue figures is shown below). Then come several pages listing all the investments held, followed by the Report of the Directors.

The latter contains a number of small items which may seem mere formalities, but are potentially very important. The directors confirm that the company still qualifies as an approved trust for tax purposes, formally announces the year's results, details substantial share interests in the company – that is, shareholders with more than 5% of the total capital – and summarises loans and donations made and proposed. The report gives details of a director retiring by rotation and seeking re-election, of directors' shareholdings and changes in them. It shows the details of the agreement between the trust and its management company, and gives formal notice of the Annual General Meeting.

Finally come ten pages of the accounts proper, made up of the Revenue Account, the Balance Sheet and the Statement of Source and Application of Funds, plus several pages of notes giving further details. We have reproduced the Revenue Account and the Balance Sheet and what follows is an explanation of any headings or notes whose significance may not be obvious.

● The Revenue Account

The Revenue Account shows where the trust's different types of revenue have come from for the one-year period leading up to the accounting date shown. It also shows what deductions have been made from them in the form of expenses, taxation and so forth, and indicates how the dividend has been arrived at.

The trust's main revenue is its income from investments. Franked and unfranked income are itemised. Note (2) to the accounts gives the breakdown of revenue between listed and unlisted investments. Interest on loans and deposits, a small amount, is the return on short-term cash deposited, for example, overnight, pending investment.

Underwriting commission is an interesting item, and one which has been gaining in importance lately because of the enormous privatisation issues which have been coming to the market. Investing institutions, including investment trusts, may be asked to underwrite part of a new share issue. That is to say, the institution will guarantee to buy a percentage of the shares should they not find buyers on the open market. In exchange for their guarantee, the institutions are paid an underwriting commission, which would usually be 1% or 1¼% of the amount involved. They get the commission even though they may not, in the end, have to lay out money for the shares.

Note (3) tells us that the interest payable was on the trust's debenture stock and 7% unsecured loan stock, though the

The Foreign and Colonial Investment Trust PLC

Revenue Account

For the year ended 31 December	Notes	1986 £'000s	£'000s	1985 £'000s	£'000s
Dividends and interest on investments	(2)				
Franked		9,789		8,768	
Unfranked		15,118		11,948	
			24,907		20,716
Interest on loans and deposits			634		621
			25,541		21,337
Underwriting commission			814		200
Other revenue			172		154
Total revenue			26,527		21,691
Interest payable and similar charges	(3)		11,208		8,015
Net revenue after interest payable			15,319		13,676
Expenses	(4)		2,024		1,676
Net revenue on ordinary activities before taxation			13,295		12,000
Taxation	(5)		4,176		3,970
Net revenue available for distribution			9,119		8,030
Dividend on preference stock			94		94
Net revenue available for ordinary shares			9,025		7,936
Dividends on ordinary shares					
Interim of 0.53p (1985–0.48p)		2,785		2,522	
Proposed final of 1.16p (1985–0.99p)		6,096		5,203	
			8,881		7,725
Amount set aside to reserves			144		211
Revenue reserve at 1 January			3,923		3,712
Revenue reserve at 31 December			4,067		3,923
Earnings per share	(6)		1.72p		1.51p

great majority of the item (£10,613,000) was on currency and sterling loans – an indication of the trust's policy on gearing.

The trust's expenses include management fees, directors' emoluments, general expenses and audit fees. By showing the total expenses figure as a percentage of the net assets figure given in the summary of results, you can see whether there has been a relative increase or decrease in management charges. For 1986, this calculation gives a ratio of 0.28%, compared to 0.33% for 1985.

The dividend on preference stock, unlike the interest on debentures and unsecured loan stock, is deducted after tax has been applied, making preference shares a much more expensive resource. The dividend on this trust's ordinary shares is paid in two instalments, which is the most usual arrangement. The two instalments are the interim – paid out mid-year – and the final – proposed in the Report and Accounts for agreement at the annual general meeting. The managers may go cautiously on the interim dividend, and make up for it with a larger final. Here, the interim of 0.53p per share and the proposed final of 1.16p add up to the 1.69p quoted in the opening summary of results.

Paying out this level of dividend does not exhaust the trust's available income, some of which is set aside to the revenue reserve. The reserve at the start of the year is shown, as well as the end of year figure, which includes the undistributed income for the year. The power to keep a revenue reserve is an advantage which investment trusts have over unit trusts. Instead of paying out the whole of incoming revenues, a reserve is put by in a good year. If there is then a slump in the amount of company dividends the trust receives in a future year, any shortfall in the trust's own dividends can be made up from its reserve. This is prticularly important for a trust which, like Foreign and Colonial, has as part of its objectives the aim to keep dividends increasing at least in line with inflation.

By looking at the difference between earnings per share and dividends per share over a period of years, you can see exactly what the trust's policy has been in terms of putting money aside to the revenue reserve. The extract below from Foreign and Colonial's ten-year revenue record shows that the trust has added to its reserve every year except for 1977, when the two figures were the same. This comparison is an indicator of how good dividends have been during the year, and how cautious the managers feel about prospects for future years.

The Foreign and Colonial Investment Trust PLC

Revenue

Year ended 31 December	1976	1977	1978	1979	1980	1981
	p	p	p	p	p	p
Earnings per share*	0.37	0.47	0.58	0.82	0.94	1.06
Dividends per share*	0.36	0.47	0.57	0.74	0.92	1.02

Year ended 31 December	1982	1983†	1984	1985	1986
	p	p	p	p	p
Earnings per share*	1.15	1.23	1.30	1.51	**1.72**
Dividends per share*	1.12	1.19	1.28	1.47	**1.69**

Adjusted to present capital

The earnings per share are arrived at by dividing £9,025,000 – the net revenue available for ordinary shares – by the 525,523,840 ordinary shares in issue, as given in note (6). Likewise, to get the dividend per share you divide the total dividend – £8,881,000 – by 525,523,840.

● The Balance Sheet

Whereas the Revenue Account effectively shows the 'housekeeping', or money in and out during the year, the balances sheet is a static view of what the trust has and what it owes at a specific date – that is, its assets and liabilities.

Tangible assets include property, office equipment and cars. Investments are broken down in note (8) to show the changes during the year: purchases, sales and the profit realised on the sales of investment holdings.

Unlisted investments are shown at directors' valuation. In other words, bcause such investments are not quoted on any stock market, there is no independent source of valuation tested by supply and demand, so they are shown in the accounts at an estimated value approved by the directors. The estimate might change from one accounting period to the next. In the most extreme circumstances, it might increase dramatically bcause the company concerned has been successfully launched in the market, or it might plummet to zero if the company goes bust.

Subsidiary companies in which the trust invests include, in this case, the Foreign and Colonial management company. In a move which was typical of the current state of the industry, Foreign and Colonial restructured its own management as a separate company in 1985.

Until then, like many old-established groups of trusts, the Foreign and Colonial trusts had been managed by a 'cooperative', which worked on a non-profitmaking basis. By setting up a separate management company, the aim was to reduce costs and make some profit from the management function by taking on other types of management, like unit trusts, offshore funds and pensions. Executives of the management company could also be rewarded with a share stake, which is likely to increase their commitment to the company, give them a personal interest in its continuing success, and hopefully secure a stable, high quality management team. The management company might well expect to seek a quotation in the future, following the successful example of other management groups like GT and Henderson.

Exchanged and forward currencies is an item that dates back to before the removal of exchange controls. Two organisations would lend each other money in different currencies. Note (9) shows that the loan agreements were set

113

The Foreign and Colonial Investment Trust PLC

Balance Sheet

At 31 December	Notes	1986 £'000s	1986 £'000s	1985 £'000s	1985 £'000s
Fixed assets					
Tangible assets	(7)		**4,001**		**4,099**
Investments	(8)				
Listed in Great Britain		262,369		194,849	
Listed outside Great Britain		540,874		369,497	
		803,243		564,346	
Unlisted at Directors' valuation		30,510		41,966	
Subsidiary companies		12,513		8,500	
			846,266		614,812
Exchanged and forward currencies	(9)		**(1,334)**		**422**
Current assets					
Debtors	(10)	11,333		4,971	
Cash at bank and in hand		668		1,203	
Short term deposits		8,026		13,712	
Taxation recoverable		6,156		4,613	
		26,183		24,499	
Current liabilities					
Creditors:					
amounts falling due within one year	(11)	**17,078**		**11,971**	
Net current assets			**9,105**		**12,528**
Total assets less current liabilities			**858,038**		**631,861**
Creditors: amounts falling due after more than one year					
Debentures and unsecured loan stock	(12)		**7,680**		**9,430**
Foreign currency and sterling loans	(13)		**139,127**		**112,473**
			711,231		**509,958**
Capital and reserves					
Called up share capital	(14)		134,071		134,071
Reserves					
Share premium	(15)	14		14	
Capital reserve	(16)	573,079		371,950	
Revenue reserve		4,067		3,923	
			577,160		375,887
			711,231		**509,958**

Approved by the board on 24 February 1987

J.R. Sclater } *Directors*
M.J. Hart

114

up in 1978, and are due to last until 1988, when the exchange will be reserved. In fact, unwinding the arrangement would result in a loss at present exchange rates, as the figure shows.

Under current assets, debtors largely consist of amounts due at the end of the Stock Exchange account following the balance sheet date. Under the account system, share bargains must be settled at the end of the two-week account period in which the deal took place.

Under the heading of Creditors: amounts falling due within one year the two largest items are investment creditors – that is, amounts due for payment at the end of the Stock Exchange account – and the proposed dividend on ordinary shares, as shown in the Revenue Account.

From the £858,038,000 total assets less current liabilities, longer term liabilities are deducted. These correspond to the repayment commitment on the gearing element of the portfolio, and again the big difference between the amount of debentures and loan stock, and the amount of currency loans is apparent.

Note (14) gives details of the company's share capital. At a mere five lines, it seems strangely insignificant given that the share capital is what originally sets the whole machine in motion! The £134,071,000 is made up largely of the ordinary shares, with the 3.5% cumulative preference stock accounting for £2,690,000.

Readers may notice that the £711,231,000 which appears, from the balance sheet, to be the net asset value, is not the same as the £708,500,000 shown in the opening summary of results. The difference between the two is the £2,690,000 preference stock. The figure in the summary deducts prior charges, which for this purpose includes preference shares.

The share premium is the extra amount paid when shares are issued at a price in excess of their face value. The capital reserve is a balancing item made up largely of unrealised surplus on investments – that is, the difference between the purchase price and what the investments were worth at the balance sheet date.

115

● Statement of Source and Application of Funds

The final major item in the accounts, which we have not shown in detail, is designed to show the source of any cash received by the investment trust during the year, and how it has been used. All sources of funds are amalgamated, so that amounts received from sales of investments and raising loans are included along with dividend income to the trust.

These 'sources' are shown against investment expenditure of various categories, including a debenture stock dated 1982/87 which has been transferred from longer term to current liabilities because its repayment is imminent. The difference between the 'sources' and 'applications' figures is expressed as an increase or a decrease (in this case a decrease) in liquidity, accounted for in this case by reductions in both bank balances and short-term deposits.

Having looked at a set of accounts in detail, what are the main things you should look out for?

● In general, look for any major changes compared to last year, and make sure they are adequately explained.

● Some changes may seem to sound warning bells, others may just be at odds with your own investment philosophy – for instance, a change in emphasis on markets or currencies which you do not agree with.

● Poor performance compared to the relevant market indices, and poor long-term performance, should make you wary.

● Increased emphasis on the unquoted element in a portfolio may be designed to put off predators, but it could also have a short-term negative effect on performance.

● It is reassuring to see independent figures, whose primary connections are outside the company, among the directors.

● Likewise, it instils confidence to see that the directors have substantial personal shareholdings in the trust, and are prepared to add to them rather than reduce them.

● Check the mix between institutional and individual shareholders. Are the institutions abandoning the trust? If so, why?

116

- Check that expenses are comparable to last year.
- Look at major changes in dividends on last year. Do they imply a change in performance, or a change in policy?
- Look out for items in the footnotes couched in jargon, and if necessary, ask the managers what they mean. For example, a large amount under 'decrease in unrealised appreciation' could mean that the directors' earlier valuation of an unlisted holding has proved to be over-optimistic.

CHAPTER TWELVE:
PORTFOLIO BUILDING

You could quite reasonably have a portfolio made up entirely of investment trusts, whether your total capital amounted to £5,000 or £100,000. A general trust with an income and growth objective and a broad geographical spread can be regarded as a complete portfolio in itself for the smaller investor with, say, up to £5,000.

If you are a first time investor, you may want to 'put a toe in the water' by investing a small part of your capital to start with. Or you may have followed investment trusts for some time, and be convinced that an investment trust portfolio is for you. In this case, you may want to put a large percentage of your free capital into investment trust shares.

If you already have a portfolio of investments, with adequate provision for emergency cash and pension, you may simply want to put all your capital into a mixed portfolio of trusts, with the emphasis on growth. If your requirements are more varied – say, for instance, that you need an income boost for a number of years following an early retirement – it may be that some other type of investment, like gilts, should be included in your portfolio, to give a high guaranteed income.

In other words, the precise nature of your financial needs will affect how much money, if any, you put into investment trust shares, which is why it is wise to seek advice. As you'll see from the case studies later in this chapter even an investment adviser specialising in investment trusts is unlikely to suggest you put all your money into this one type of investment.

The following is a guide to the type of portfolio you might

consider, depending on the amount of capital you have available:

● **£10,000 or less:**

holdings in one or two well-spread general trusts with good track records.

● **£10,000 to £50,000:**

several holdings, still with the emphasis on general trusts, though beginning to develop a wider spread of investments. For instance, some with more overseas emphasis, some invested primarily in the UK. Relatively high or low yields to be chosen depending on income requirements and tax position.

● **£50,000 and more:**

a portfolio still based on general trusts, though with a limited number of holdings from specialist sectors, bearing in mind that these are relatively more volatile, and market timing of your investments is crucial.

Meeting your objectives

As the above comments indicate, there are a number of questions to ask yourself about your investment requirements before you start to choose an investment trust portfolio. How much do you want to invest? Are you mainly interested in income or growth? Do you want primarily a UK investment or a broader geographical spread?

As for the trust itself, you will obviously want to look at past performance of both net asset value — indicating how good the managers are — and share price — showing how the market has favoured the trusts; the discount; the record of the management group; the category in which the trust is listed; the recent trading range of the share price (from the *Financial Times*, for example), and the most recent geographical spread (from the AITC's MIS).

Armed with a number of criteria based on a little preliminary reviewing of your objectives, it is surprising how you can whittle down the difficult task of choosing a trust from the large number available.

Some typical cases

To give some idea of how you might make use of investment trusts in your portfolio, we have drawn up three case studies which show investors with different requirements, for all of whom an investment trust element would be attractive. The idea is to give some practical examples of the considerations which are important in planning this sort of portfolio. You will see that in two out of three cases, investment trusts are not the *only* type of investment suggested. Most people have a number of different investment needs, and usually these cannot be met by a single investment.

I am grateful to the Bell Lawrie White private client service for providing details of the cases which follow. Though the people described are fictitious, they are based on typical clients of the service.

● The sceptical businessman

Forty-eight-year-old Andrew Ritch is a self-made man. Having started his working life as a trainee with the electricity board, he eventually left to set up his own business, which he built up successfully over a number of years. However, sorting out his own finances fills him with dread, and he feels intimidated by insurance brokers and investment consultants.

Andrew sold his business recently to Widget plc for £200,000 in cash, and £100,000 of Widget shares which he cannot sell for five years. Widget employs him to manage the business with a salary of £30,000 a year – similar to his takings from the business for the last two years.

Andrew is married with two children aged fourteen and twelve, both at the local state school. He reckons his house is now worth £140,000, and he has a £30,000 mortgage backed by a with-profits endowment policy which matures in 1999. He has been making contributions to a self-employed pension scheme, and is now joining his new employer's scheme. He has a £50,000 capital gains tax bill from the sale of his business, which falls due in December 1987.

120

'I'm not worried for the present about income,' said Andrew in his discussion with the private client service, 'as I think my new salary, plus the bonuses, and the dividends on my Widget shares, should be enough to cover our outgoings. I can't see that this whacking great CGT bill is right, though. The wife and I worked ourselves into the ground to build up Ritch Fittings from nothing, and that is a great chunk of the benefit just wiped out. And now you tell me that if I have a heart attack tomorrow, there would be an inheritance tax bill as well!'

The talk with Mr Ritch was ticklish going at the time. He had had difficulty in meeting the payments on a previous mortgage, and had been incensed when he found out he could not roll up the interest, because of the insurance link. He felt the insurance salesman had sold him the wrong policy, and his strong dislike of nearly all financial institutions dates from about this time.

The feelings about insurance brokers which he expressed at the meeting do not bear repeating. 'I do not go knocking on people's doors getting them to have their house rewired when all they need is a new plug,' he fulminated.

The arrangements eventually agreed for him had the advantage of simplicity, and they went some way towards reducing the potential inheritance tax bill which, as far as he was concerned, was the last straw. He would not have to worry about his money day to day, and it could be easily realised at any time, since it would not be tied up in a complicated insurance scheme.

First of all, the £50,000 earmarked for the CGT bill was put on one side in a low coupon short-dated gilt. Then the inheritance tax arrangements: Mr Ritch would give £50,000 to his wife, who would use the funds to set up an accumulation and maintenance trust for the children. Mr Ritch would himself set up a similar trust, using another £50,000. Gifts between husband and wife, of course, do not incur inheritance tax, and neither do the gifts into the accumulation and maintenance trusts, provided Mr Ritch manages to stave off his heart attack for seven years. ('I think you'd better take up jogging, dear,' sniggered Mrs Ritch.)

When the Widget shares can be sold, he could consider making a further gift to the children. In the meantime, he would invest the remaining £50,000.

Investment trusts were discussed as a home for his own portfolio, as well as for the two accumulation and maintenance trusts. He liked the idea of investing in the stock market at a discount. I've always used discount promotions to build up good relations with my customers, so that idea really appeals.' He also approved of the low charges − 'A darn sight cheaper than my bank quoted me for their discretionary management service.'

He was pleased to hear that investment trusts were not themselves liable to tax on their capital gains, but accepted that he might incur a tax bill on the gains made on selling his own investment trust shareholdings. The arrangements were made still simpler by using the same trusts for each portfolio − which meant fewer trusts for him to follow. Five trusts were chosen with well diversified trusts with good long-term records, which between them would give Andrew Ritch a good spread of international markets.

● The modest widow

Prudence Cash is a sixty-two-year-old widow who lives in a council house. As well as her state pension, she gets a small pension from her late husband's employers. Her mother left her £25,000 when she died recently, and she is looking for advice on how to invest it.

True to her name, Prudence has an old-fashioned knack of 'making do' on her income. The new captal is not needed, therefore, to help with day-to-day essentials, or to provide new comforts. She does not want, and could not cope with, a big change in her lifestyle.

What she *would* like is to be able to visit her family more often than at present. Her home is in Manchester, but her children have long since flown the nest. Her sons went to London to look for better job prospects, and her daughter, married to a leading seaman in the Royal Navy, lives in Plymouth.

All Prudence wants from her investments is enough income to enable her to travel south more often, and to indulge her seven grandchildren with better Christmas and birthday presents.

'It's the train fares that are the problem,' says Prudence. 'Do you know what the return fare to Plymouth is nowadays? I'm sure you could go to America for less than that when I was young. And the worst of it is, they keep going up.' When pressed to give an idea of her needs, she said she thought £1,000 a year should cover it. To start with, though, she wanted to take £2,000 of the capital for more ambitious travel plans – to visit her sister in Australia whom she has not seen for twelve years.

Prudence's original thought had been to put her money into the building society. She is very shrewd at weighing up the best-paying accounts available, and had one all lined up. She worked out that she could get almost £2,000 in interest, and thought she would just let the extra roll up.

Then she read an article in the paper which put doubt in her mind about the tax position if she kept so much money in the building society. A friend's son in the financial world put her in touch with the Bell Lawrie White service.

During their discussion with her, various points were made. First, though interest rates were high at the time she was thinking of investing, even after taking inflation into account, this situation may not last for ever. Her income requirements are bound to increase over the years, and Prudence, who looks more like fifty-two than sixty-two, could have at least another twenty years or more of retirement to provide for. In other words, keeping her income at a constant level – or preferably, increasing it in order to help fight inflation – is more important for her than being absolutely sure that her capital will not go down in value.

Prudence had also been quite right to think about the tax implications. The interest on a standard building society deposit comes with basic rate tax already paid but under new regulations if Prudence informs the society that she is a non-taxpayer she can receive her interest gross.

The investment income in the portfolio suggested to Prudence is taxable, of course, but since it is arranged to give her the amount she needs, without an excess, the tax impact should not be so heavy. If she had another large one-off expense like her trip to Australia, she could also sell some of her investments within the annual CGT limit, and get a boost to her income which was effectively tax free.

In any case, the suggestions from the private client service included putting £1,000 into the building society for emergency use. Prudence felt happy about this, as it meant she could lay her hands on some cash just a short walk from home at her local branch. It was suggested that £8,000 should go into long dated government stocks – 'gilts' – because these ensure a constant high income, and some possibility of capital growth.

The bulk of the portfolio was to be divided between three investment trusts giving an average starting yield of 6%. Prudence was not impressed with this figure until it was explained to her that it should grow as time went on. All the trusts chosen had impressive records for growth of dividends, and this was expected to continue. Of course, there were good prospects for capital gain as well, although this could not be guaranteed.

● The redundant distiller

Adrian McLuker, aged thirty-four, was made redundant three months ago by the distillery where he had worked since leaving university. Luckily, he found a new job pretty quickly as sales director with a brewing company.

He has done well from the change: his new salary is £18,000 plus bonus plus car. His wife also works, earning £8,000 a year as a secretary at an advertising agency. They have a £26,000 mortgage on their house, no immediate plans to start a family, and capital of £30,000 in redundancy money from Adrian's previous job.

124

'They do say redundancy can sometimes be the best thing to happen to you, and I feel that's true in my own case,' said Adrian. 'I've now got the capital to build up a really good lump sum which will increase the family's financial security in the future, and I feel we're young enough to be able to take some risks.'

With his new job involving quite a bit of travelling, both in the UK and on the continent, Adrian had already decided that the best type of investment would be a managed fund of some sort. 'My new job's going to take up all my energies and more, and I don't want to have to watch share prices like a hawk from day to day, but on the other hand I want to feel I'm not getting a boringly cautious investment. I'd like to put the whole lot into some sort of stock market vehicle. We already have a £2,000 contingency fund in the building society.'

One of his former colleagues at the distillery, made redundant a year before Adrian, had become a life insurance salesman (or 'consultant', as he liked to describe himself). This friend had suggested Adrian put all his capital into a unit-linked bond. Adrian asked his bank manager for his views, and was advised not to commit himself too quickly to an insurance related product, but to keep his funds in cash until he had found a new job, and then look at unit trusts.

This seemed like sense to Adrian, who, on reading the literature, felt the taxation of the bond to be a disadvantage, and bond performance generally to be less good than unit trusts. He had come to the private client service for suggestions on a unit trust portfolio.

One of Adrian's stipulations was that part of his portfolio should be in Japan and the Far East. He had visited this part of the world while working for the distillery, and felt the growth prospects were outstanding: 'You've got to take your hat off to them. They're terrifyingly efficient, and do they know about financial controls! And it's not just the Japs. There's plenty of up-and-coming economies in that part of the world. We certainly haven't heard the last of them.'

He paused for breath when it was pointed out to him that, though unit trusts are an excellent investment for specialist

125

overseas markets, you could, at the time he was looking to invest, buy investment trusts specialising in Japan and the Far East on discounts of 15% or more to current assets.

A long discussion ensued about the significance of the discount and the differences between investment trusts and unit trusts. His reaction was, 'If investment trusts are as good as you say, I'm surprised I haven't read more about them.' The limitations on marketing investment trusts were explained to him. The arguments in favour of them were backed up by statistics showing that the average investment trust tends to outperform not only the average unit trust over most periods, but the FT Actuaries All Share Index as well.

Adrian was convinced, and asked for suggestions for the investment of the full lump sum in investment trusts, with capital appreciation as the main objective. Compared to an insurance bond, of course, the tax position with this sort of portfolio would be much simpler. There would not be a great deal of income tax to pay cn the relatively low-yielding trusts chosen, and he and his family could simply forget about their portfolio for a few years, or take profits as the need arose, avoiding a tax bill by staying within the CGT exempt limit.

The portfolio recommended consisted of five trusts, with one trust specially chosen to cater for his Far Eastern investment needs.

CHAPTER THIRTEEN:
THE PREDATORS SWOOP

The investment trust industry changed very fast in the eighties bull market with companies being taken over or turned into unit trusts. The UK stock market was suffering from takeover mania with more and more companies looking to acquisitions as a quick route to growth. Some investment trusts were taken over by investment companies which were seeking to increase funds under management and some by industrial firms wanting to unlock cheap assets if the trust's shares were standing at a substantial discount to the value of its holdings. Although the nineties have started on a quieter note, the long-term prospect of renewed take-over activity should not be ruled out. As and when the stock market revives investment trusts could be a relatively cheap way for institutions to buy well-balanced portfolios.

Attractive targets

Why are investment trusts so attractive as takeover targets for industrial companies, and why are such takeovers regarded as a good thing for investors? The key to the whole matter lies in the discount. When a trust portfolio is sold the price received for the shares will equal the trust's net asset value minus transaction costs. In other words, each share in the investment trust company suddenly becomes worth nearly net asset value, whereas before the bid it could have traded at a significant discount. This has obvious benefits for the investor, but the bidder will also do quite well by agreeing to reimburse the shareholders while making a few percentage points profit as well.

The object of the exercise as far as the bidder is concerned is to turn the portfolio into cash. If he can do so on a large portfolio and make even two or three per cent for himself, he is effectively making an instant profit.

The trust might be standing at a 20% discount. If the bidder offers shareholders 95% of the net asset value, he is still earning 5% for himself. This sort of deal has often proved irresistible to institutional shareholders who, though they might support the trust concerned, cannot justify turning down profit on such a scale.

Shareholder's strategy

Where there is a takeover, the investor is usually offered two choices: either he can sell his shares for cash to the bidding company, which might be worth 95% of net asset value, or swap them for shares in the bidding company itself, which might be pitched at the equivalent of 102% of net asset value.

In practice a 'formula net asset value' is established, and the offers made to shareholders will be expressed as a percentage of that. Formula net asset value will take into account all the expenses of disposal, including the repayment of loans, debentures and preference stocks, the dealing expenses relating to the sale of the portfolio, and any additional costs such as severance pay to employees and cancellation of the management contract.

The decision on whether to take cash or accept the bidder's shares will largely depend upon your perception of the future fortunes of the bidding company. There is also a tax angle to consider. If the investment trust shareholdings are switched into shares in the bidding company, no disposal is regarded as having taken place for capital gains tax purposes. Taking the cash offer, on the other hand, does count as a disposal, and may make the investor liable to capital gains tax.

A takeover of an investment trust by an industrial company is usually described as a 'disguised rights issue'. This means that the bidder company is raising cash without approaching its existing shareholders who, it may feel, would not support a request for further funds.

Most popular takeover targets have been general trusts

where the portfolio is largely in major shares which are easy to sell. Also vulnerable are trusts with a poor performance record whose shares stand at a large discount to net asset value. It used to be thought that size was some protection against a takeover, but the acquisition of Philip Hill, which weighed in at more than £350m, has proved this view wrong.

Takeover bids are also made occasionally by one investment trust for another. In this case the motivation is honest empire-building. The bidding trust will simply be seeking to increase the funds it has under management. A bid by one trust for another will have to be carefully timed. The bidding trust's shares should be at a narrower discount than the target trust's shares, or even standing at a premium, in order for its shares to be an attractive alternative for the target trust's shareholders.

Winding-up

Some investment trust companies are set up for a limited timespan, as in the case of split-level trusts. This provides investors with an additional degree of certainty, since they know that at a specific date in the future they will be given the true net asset value of each share, minus a small sum for transaction costs. This means that as the winding-up date approaches the trust's shares tend to trade at or near net asset value.

When a split level trust is wound up, the capital shareholders will usually be offered shares in a new investment trust or an interest in a new unit trust as an alternative to receiving cash. This is arguably the best way of winding up a trust, since it avoids an immediate capital gains tax liability and gives shareholders a similar investment with similar policies to their original holdings.

The table shows those split level trusts with fixed winding up dates and gives details of their capital shares. The share price information, discount or premium are as at 31 December 1990. This information is updated each month in the MIS, published by the AITC.

129

Split Level Trusts

Trust	Share price p	Discount % – premium	Winding-up Date
City and Commercial	120	11	1988-1/2/1993
Exmoor Dual	35	44	31/8/2001
General Consolidated	92	34	31/12/1997
Mezzanine	68	–	fr. 1/12/2001
New Throgmorton (1983)	55	55	fr. 25/7/1991
Rights & Issues	265	–	fr. 25/7/1991
River & Merc. Amercian	17	45	28/12/1999
River & Merc Geared	18	30	fr. 30/9/199
River & Mercantile	86	29	30/4/2000
River Plate & General	58	50	31/10/1996
Scottish National	45	−22	30/9/1998
Throgmorton Dual	290	51	31/121999
Triplerest	1385	8	28/2/1991
Yeoman	121	10	fr. 30/9/1992

Source: MIS (January 1991)

CHAPTER FOURTEEN:
QUESTIONS AND ANSWERS

1 *Investment trusts seem very complicated. Wouldn't I be better going for something simpler?*
It's true that investment trusts have some technical aspects which are hard to understand, though, as with motor cars, once you've learnt how to handle them, you don't need to know exactly how the machinery works. The basic principles are really very simple: there are no limitations on how much you can invest or for how long. You can check the value of your investment daily. You can sell all or part of your investment trust holding whenever you like and get your money back quickly. The costs involved are the same as buying other shares like British Telecom. The tax position is straightforward. A non-taxpayer can reclaim the tax paid on dividends, and it is easy, with a bit of planning to avoid capital gains tax. Like other packaged share schemes, trusts should be considered as a long-term investment.

2 *If investment trusts are so good, why haven't I heard about them before?*
Investment trusts are companies and so they cannot advertise their shares to the public, except when the shares are sold for the first time, i.e. a new issue. This means that promoting the virtues of any single investment trust is difficult. The industry as a whole through the Association of Investment Trust Companies promotes the benefits of owning shares in investment trust companies. At the time of writing there were signs that investment trusts might be more actively marketed in the future as the regulators considered giving companies the opportunity to cold-call investors

3 What is the minimum amount you can invest in an investment trust?

There is technically no minimum amount, you could buy one share if you wanted to, though you would pay many times the share price in commission. Even after Big Bang, most stockbrokers are sticking to the old minimum commission levels. Typically, you might expect to pay a fee of £25.00 for a small bargain of £1,000. Some regional stockbrokers and no-frill share services may be cheaper but they may charge a joining fee and impose certain dealing restrictions. You might, therefore, regard £1,000 as an acceptable minimum, or you may be prepared to pay this scale of fees on, say, £700 or £800. Of course, you can invest much less than this through a regular savings plan, most of which have a £25 a month minimum, without incurring heavy charges.

4 How long should I hold on to my investment trust shares?

We've said a number of times that investment trusts are a long-term investment, but the answer to this question will depend on what sort of investor you are, what ultimate use you want to put your money to, what sort of trusts you have invested in, and stock market conditions during the life of your shareholding.

Generally speaking you should regard two or three years as the minimum period for investing in a general trust but if you choose a specialist trust, for example one where your money is invested in gold, you may need to be more nimble to maximise your profit. You certainly should not put money into investment trusts when you know you are going to need it within, say, six months. You can, of course, hold on to investment trust shares for as long as you want, unless the trust has a fixed winding up date at which time you will be repaid the value of your shares.

5 How quickly can I get my money back?

Shares in investment trusts companies quoted on the London Stock Exchange, are subject to the exchange's account system. The Stock Exchange year is divided into twenty-four periods known as accounts, usually of two weeks' duration. Dealings within each account are paid for on the settlement day, which is the second Monday after the account ends. In other words, if you instruct your stockbroker to sell on the first day of the account, you might wait almost four weeks for your money, while if you sold on the last day of the account you would receive your cash in ten days.

6 *Isn't there a lot of paperwork involved in investment trusts?*
There are a number of documents involved in buying and selling shares in investment trust companies just as with any shares. If you have three or four holdings, and stick with them long term, this should not be too onerous. Remember to keep all the relevant papers in a safe place and keep a note of purchases, sales and dividends so you have all the necessary information to hand for filling in your tax return.

If you deal very frequently the paper starts to mount up in which case you might prefer to ask your stockbroker to handle the paperwork for you.

7 *When and how is income paid?*
The majority of investment trust companies pay dividends twice a year, though some pay four times a year, and some only once. The dividend is paid to you by cheque along with a tax voucher showing that income tax has been deducted at the basic rate. You will need these details for your tax return. If you prefer, you can have your dividends paid direct to your bank account, by completing a dividend mandate form from the company concerned.

8 *Why do shares sell at a discount?*
A good question. Even within the industry you will find a number of explanations put forward. These include the following: the discount is there because you are buying, as it were, a collection of shares at one remove – you can't readily realise their full net asset value, and even in the best of worlds the discount would reflect the costs of selling the portfolio. You are also buying a pool of shares rather than a single share, so the future prospects are that much harder to predict. Some also suggest that discounts exist because there is an over-supply of investment trust shares or the investment trust company's track record is bad.

Whatever the truth of these views, you can also look at it another way. Given that the share price itself is affected by many factors such as management expertise, supply and demand, and the view of the markets in which the trust is invested, it would be a surprising coincidence if the share price and the current net asset value of the trust were exactly the same. Generally, share prices tend to reflect investors' view of a company's future rather than its current worth.

9 *Investment trusts are a relic of the nineteenth century. Aren't they really rather old-fashioned?*

When the oldest trust in existence, Foreign and Colonial, has invested in controversial new ventures like The Independent newspaper and Eurotunnel, as well as having pathfinding investments in emerging markets like Brazil and Korea, and in addition to all this produced 40% net asset growth during 1986, no one can say that its long history is a disadvantage. Most people would be happy with an old-fashioned investment that performed so well!

10 *I've heard it's hard to make very large funds perform. Do the larger trusts tend to do badly?*

It is not true that large investment trusts are bound to perform badly, though some large trusts do have a better record than others. There is no cast-iron relationship between size and performance. While size is no bar to good performance, an individual trust's record is the best guide. It is also vital that you choose the right type of trust to suit your needs, i.e. income or capital and consider the investment sector carefully.

11 *I'm interested in investing for the first time. What sort of trust should I choose?*

Assuming you are a first-time investor starting off with a fairly small sum and are prepared to leave the money invested for a few years, you would probably do best to start with a broadly spread generalist trust which has a reasonable yield and a consistent performance record in the top half of its category. Start looking among the Capital and Income Growth: General trusts.

12 *Would an investment trust be a good financial gift for a child?*

Yes, excellent! A generalist trust will give you a well-spread pool of shareholdings which can be held for an infant until the age of eighteen, but can be partly or wholly encashed in the meantime if necessary.

Parents should give very low-yielding trusts, or the capital shares of a split capital trust, as they will be liable for the income tax on their own gifts. Anyone else making a gift to a child need not worry about this, as there will be no tax to pay unless the child's total income is higher than the tax-free personal allowance, which is announced each year in the Budget. Investment trust regular savings plans are ideal ways of saving for children as well.

13 *Is it always best to go for the trust with the largest discount?*

No. It depends on why the trust is at a discount. If it is simply that the market is out of favour, and is sure to return to popularity shortly, a big discount can be a definite advantage. This situation existed with trusts invested in the Japanese stock market at the end of 1986. No one regarded them globally as a poor sector, but the market was temporarily out of favour. Discounts widened for a short period to around 30% in some cases, but were narrowing progressively within a month or two.

It may be that a trust is on a wide discount because it has a poor performance record and shows no sign of improvement, or because it is in a sector which appears to be stuck in the doldrums for the foreseeable future. In this case, buying on a large discount could be a bad idea – unless, of course, you are prepared to gamble on the possibility of the trust changing its objectives for a more successful policy or being taken over.

14 *I've heard it said that you can't lose at present with investment trusts, because if the trust doesn't perform well it will get taken over. Is this true?*

This is the somewhat jocular 'dartboard' theory which was voiced in the heady optimism of the eighties. The idea was you threw a dart at the investment trust list, and even if you came up with a poor performer, the chances were it would be taken over, and you would get an excellent return once the assets were realised.

My reaction? Don't bank on it! For most fairly small investors, a more conservative approach to investment is desirable, so choose a trust which has some past performance record. Choosing a trust because you expect it to be taken over is risky at the best of times, but specially if your only research is a set of 'arrows'.

15 Are takeovers good or bad for the investment trust shareholder?

Takeovers are usually thought of as a quick way to a tidy profit for the investment trust shareholder, because you are likely to realise well over 90% of the trust's net asset value per share. You will usually be given the choice between cash and shares in the company which is making the bid. Which choice turns out to be the better will depend ultimately on the performance of the bidding company's shares.

16 How can I pick out trusts which are takeover prospects?

It's difficult for the private investor to compete with the professionals in this area. By the time there is any concrete news in the press on possible takeover moves, the price of the trust being bid for will probably already have risen. To make the right choice as a private investor is, as we've said above, a gamble, and there is no magic formula other than reading all you can about the investment trust market and making an informed guess.

17 Why is no p/e ratio ever quoted for investment trusts?

P/e (price/earnings) ratios are used as a guide to the market's expectations of a particular company's future earnings capacity. The ratio is arrived at by dividing the company's share price by the earnings per share. The result tells you how fast profits are expected to rise in the near future: the higher the p/e, the more earnings are expected to rocket.

Investment trusts are rather different from most other quoted companies, and, in spite of the discount, their share prices are usually quite closely related to changes in net asset

136

values. Earnings are relatively less important than with an industrial company. If you do a p/e calculation for an investment trust, you will get results in the 50s, 60s or 70s, which is sky-high in terms of the UK stock market, and suggests a high-risk 'hot stock' which is really expected to go places. This is obviously not the image of most investment trusts, which emphasise steady rather than meteoric growth, so the p/e ratio is redundant.

18 *How well can an investment trust protect your investment in a bear market?*

The returns on any equity investment will reflect the fortunes of the market in which it is invested. The same is true of direct share investments, investment trusts, unit trusts, or insurance bonds. If there is a severe and prolonged bear market no manager, however good, will be able to keep the trust's assets on a rising curve.

The first move a manager would make in such market conditions would be to reduce borrowings – as we have seen, gearing enhances downward as well as upward share price movements. An investment trust manager's capital is fixed, so he can take a long-term view, often picking up some very good bargains at the bottom of the market which will give excellent performance once the index rises again.

The problem of bear markets is one reason why investors really should regard investment trust shares as long-term investments. During a bear market those who have to sell their shares fare very badly. Those who are able to hold on usually recoup lost ground in the long term. It is not often that such severe market conditions occur worldwide. It is part of an investment manager's task to try and anticipate which markets are at the start of a bear phase and switch into those which are rising.

19 *Why should anyone accept the relatively unexciting gain on a loan stock, knowing the ordinary shareholders are increasing their gains at his expense?*

The house mortgage comparison is useful in answering this one. Why does the building society lend money to buy houses for a rate of interest, when it could actually buy the houses and get much higher levels of capital growth? The answer is that the building society doesn't want a return in ten or twenty years' time. It is in business to pay interest on lenders' savings, so it needs a constant flow of interest income to meet its day-to-day liabilities. With an investment trust, the position is not dissimilar. The holders of loan stock tend to be institutions rather than individual investors. They will mostly be organisations like pension funds and insurance companies which have to find a certain level of regular income to make payments to pensioners or annuity holders. They are therefore happy to take a guaranteed regular return.

20 Which are best: unit trusts or investment trusts?
There has traditionally been a bitter battle between the proponents of unit trusts and investment trusts, though nowadays some brokers are beginning to see the two types of investment as complementary. One of the greatest bones of contention is that traditionally unit trusts pay a higher rate of commission to brokers, 3% compared to 1.65%, and there is therefore an incentive to recommend unit trusts rather than investment trusts. It is the customer who ends up footing the bill for the charges.

What are the main differences between the two?

● An investment trust is a quoted company, and the investor buys shares. A unit trust is a trust fund, and the investor buys units.

● Investment trust shares are bought through a stockbroker. Units are bought through a unit trust broker or directly from the management group.

● Investment trusts usually sell at a discount to net asset value. Unit trust prices are directly related to net asset value in an agreed formula laid down by the Department of Trade and Industry.

● An investment trust has a fixed capital structure. Units in a unit trust can be created or liquidated according to demand. This means an investment trust manager can take a much longer term view than a unit trust manager, because he will not have to sell investment in order to redeem shares.

• Management expenses on investment trusts are usually much lower than on unit trusts: 0.4% or less per annum compared to 1½%.

• Dealing costs are less with an investment trust, which has only a 2% spread and commission of 1.65% or less, compared to the 6%-7% spread on a standard general unit trust.

• Investment trusts can borrow to increase the funds under their management. Unit trusts cannot.

• There are many more unit trusts than investment trusts, with a wide range of highly specialised funds.

• Unit trusts are able to advertise freely. Investment trusts are currently more tightly regulated.

• Short-term unit trust performance is widely quoted in the press, and unit trust managers are criticised for encouraging a shorter and shorter view of their investment. Investment trusts tend to concentrate on their steady growth record over a long period.

What does all this add up to? What are the advantages and disadvantages? Investment trusts are at an advantage in being a bit cheaper to buy and sell, and a lot cheaper in terms of annual management charges. The discount can also be an advantage in many cases, especially if it allows you to get into an out-of-favour market at a bargain price, whereas a unit trust's price will always be close to net asset value. On the other hand, if a market is much in depand and most trusts investing in it are at a premium, then a unit trust may offer a cheaper way in.

Investment trusts tend to have a consistent performance record. You can pick out trusts which have stayed high up in their sector ranking over many years. With unit trusts, it is much harder to find such consistency.

21 *What is the tax position on any profits I make from my investment trust company shares?*
When you buy shares you must remember that there are two types of return which might generate a tax liability. You will be liable to income tax on all the dividend income you receive

from your shares. This will be paid to you net of basic rate tax. Higher rate taxpayers will have an additional bill and non-taxpayers can reclaim the tax paid on their behalf. If you pay tax at the basic rate you will not need to pay any more.

In addition, there are the capital gains that you may make to consider, i.e. the profits on the actual sale of your shares. These profits are liable to capital gains tax but in practice few investors pay this tax. That's because most people find their annual capital gains tax allowance exceeds their investment profits in the tax year.

22 *The investment trust company I am considering as part of my portfolio is according to my adviser 'approved'. What does this mean?*

The term approved has nothing whatever to do with the merits or otherwise of the trust's investment performance. Basically in exchange for fulfilling certain requirements an approved investment trust obtains certain tax benefits. The main requirements for approval are that the company be resident in the UK, listed on the Stock Exchange, derives its income wholly or mainly from shares, does not invest more than 15% of its assets in any one company (except another investment trust), it must not retain more than 15% of its income and capital gains made from the sale of investments must not be distributed as dividends. Provided these criteria are met, the main tax advantage for the investment trust company is that profits it makes on investment sales are not liable to capital gains tax. Given the size and scope of investment trust companies' activities this concession is very valuable.

CHAPTER FIFTEEN:
GLOSSARY

Active management
A fund is said to be actively managed if the manager is prepared to make big changes in emphasis between markets or sectors, and to move frequently if necessary. Active management is not necessarily better than a more passive approach. It implies an aggressive investment philosophy and may indicate a higher risk trust.

Asset allocation
The way in which a trust's investments are spread across world markets and sectors. A change from being 50% to 35% invested in the UK is an asset allocation decision.

Association of Investment Trust Companies (AITC)
The trade association to which most quoted investment trusts belong, and part of whose task is to inform the public about the benefits of investment trusts. The Association's address is Park House (6th Floor), 16 Finsbury Circus, London EC2M 7JJ; Tel: 071-588 5347

B shares
A class of ordinary share which, instead of providing a dividend, gives holders an annual scrip issue of additional shares. Originally designed as a tax-efficient investment for the higher rate taxpayer, the benefits of B shares were removed by legislation in 1975.

Back-to-back loans
A type of currency loan transaction used to hedge the

currency exposure of a portfolio. A UK trust will lend an amount in sterling to a UK subsidiary of, say, a US bank. The parent company then lends dollars to the trust.

Bid price
The lower of the two prices quoted for shares. The bid price is what you get back when you sell, so you should always value your investment on a bid price basis.

Big Bang
This is the title given to the sweeping changes which took place in the London Stock Exchange in October 1986. The main changes were that the traditional broker and jobber system disappeared, and a minimum commission level on share dealings was abolished. Dealings have become cheaper for institutional investors like investment trusts, but not necessarily for the private individual.

Bonus issue
Also called a scrip issue or capitalisation issue, a bonus issue is when the company gives to each shareholder, free of charge, a number of new shares for each share he or she already holds. After the bonus issue, the company's share price is likely to fall to reflect the number of new shares issued.

Bought deal
A jargon term associated with investment trust takeovers. If an investment trust predator makes a successful bid, it may want to realise the trust's assets as quickly and as profitably as possible by selling them all in one go to another organisation, which will then dispose of them in the market. Interested organisations will offer to dispose of the portfolio, and the sale is described as a bought deal.

Break-up basis
The most conservative formula for calculating net asset value, by deducting prior charges at their redemption value (see prior charges).

Capital shares
In a split capital trust, the shares which get the benefit of all, or most, of the capital appreciation on the trust's portfolio.

Capital structure
The different amounts and types of stocks and shares which go to make up a trust's capital – the amount of ordinary and preference shares, debentures and unsecured loan stock, etc, which are in issue.

Capitalisation issue (see Scrip issue)

Commission
The charge made by a stockbroker on a share transaction. (See also Underwriting commission.)

Concentration
The number of different shareholdings in a portfolio. The fewer held, the more concentrated the portfolio is said to be.

Convertibles
Stock which carries a fixed rate of interest, but has the right to be converted into ordinary shares at some time in the future. You may find the expressions 'convertibles converted/ not converted', which refers to the formula used to calculate net asset value – assuming that the convertibles in issue either have or have not been converted into ordinary shares.

Cumulative
When referring to loan stock or shares, cumulative means that if the payment due for one period is missed, those securities must be given priority when the next payment is made, and arrears of the missed amounts must be paid before any dividend can be paid on the ordinary shares. Cumulative preference shares and cumulative unsecured loan stock (CULS) are often mentioned.

Currency loan
A loan taken out by an investment trust where the money borrowed is in a foreign currency.

Currency swap
A transaction used to hedge currency exposure whereby a UK and an overseas organisation agree to swap similar amounts of currencies at current rates of exchange, and to re-exchange them at the same rates at a specified date in the future.

Debenture stock
A type of loan capital with a fixed annual rate of interest and repayment value. Debenture stockholders take precedence over ordinary and preference shareholders in the event of an investment trust company being wound up. Debenture stocks are one of the commonest traditional forms of long-term borrowing. Debenture stocks are usually 'secured' on the company's assets and therefore have a prior claim to repayment over unsecured creditors.

Debt structure
The amount and type of different classes of debt a trust may have. This includes loan capital and foreign currency loans.

Deferred shares
These are a type of ordinary share which receive no dividend either for an initial specified period or until the ordinary share dividend reaches a certain level.

Development capital
A form of venture finance where the capital is required for developing, rather than setting up, a business. Investment trusts specialising in unquoteds may offer this type of capital to young companies.

Directors' valuation
Assets shown on the balance sheet at directors' valuation are unquoted companies where no market value can be quoted. The trust's directors therefore value such a company as best they can depending on its current health and prospects.

Discount
If the share price of an investment trust is lower than the net asset value per share, the trust is said to be trading at a discount. The discount is shown as a percentage of the net asset value (see also Premium).

Disguised rights issue
This is another term from the jargon of takeovers. If a company wants to raise new capital, but is not well enough regarded in the market for a new issue of its own shares to be a success, an alternative might be to take over an

investment trust. Realising the trust's assets provides the necessary cash, and the company concerned does not have to approach its shareholders directly for the new money.

Diversified portfolio
A portfolio of investments which is widely spread across a number of different markets or sectors, without a dominant emphasis in one particular area.

Dividend
The income from a share investment. Most companies pay dividends twice a year. The mid-year payment is known as the interim, and the end-of-year payment as the final. Dividends may be quoted gross – that is, before any deduction of tax in the hands of the shareholder – or net – after deduction of basic rate tax – which is how dividends are paid.

Dual capital trust
A trust where the share capital is split between capital shares, which attract all or most of the capital growth, and income shares, which receive all the income. The idea is to offer shares which are tax-efficient for different types of investor. Dual capital trusts are also known as split capital or dual purpose trusts.

Dual purpose trust (see Dual capital trust)

E.P.S.
Earnings per share. Usually calculated on the basis of pre-tax profits and issued share capital.

Equity capital
The capital provided by the ordinary shareholders, who collectively own the company, and benefit from capital growth if the share price rises, as well as dividends. The equity shareholders have least security, coming last in the order of preference if the company is wound up.

Equity participation
Holding a share in the company's equity capital. An investment trust management group may be spun off as a separate company partly in order to give the executives equity participation, and hence a chance to share in the company's future growth.

Exchange controls

Abolished in 1979, exchange controls existed to inhibit overseas investment, making it difficult and expensive for companies to obtain foreign currency. Following their abolition, there has been a considerable surge in overseas investment. The legislation which established exchange controls is being removed from the statute book.

Exposure

The amount of a portfolio invested in a particular area. If you have £10,000, and £5,000 of it is invested overseas, you are said to have a 50% overseas exposure. Currency exposure is the amount of a portfolio which is vulnerable to exchange rate fluctuations in a specific currency. For example, if a trust is 50% invested in the US, and has no hedging, it is 50% exposed to the dollar. Trusts use hedging to reduce their currency exposure if they expect adverse exchange rate movements.

Final (see Dividend)

Financial futures contract

Futures contracts are agreements to buy or sell commodities at an agreed price by an agreed date in the future. Such contracts are dealt in on futures markets in major financial centres. In the case of financial futures, the commodity is currencies, interest rates or stock market indices. Contracts like these are an easy and flexible means of hedging.

Fixed interest securities

Securities which, like debenture stocks and loan stocks, carry a fixed rate of interest, called a coupon. They also have a redemption value, which is the amount repaid at the redemption date. The market price may range above or below the redemption (or par) value. Most such securities have a fixed redemption date, or a time period within which they must be redeemed. In the wider market, fixed interest securities include British government stocks (gilts), and all types of corporate or government bond.

Formula net asset value
This is the estimated net asset value per share fixed by the
bidding company when making a bid for an investment trust.
This value is varied during the course of a bid in the light of
subsequent price movements.

Forward exchange contract (see Financial futures contract)

Franked income
UK share dividends are franked income in the hands of an
investment trust. That is, they are paid to the trust out of
company revenue after corporation tax has been deducted.
They are therefore regarded as 'tax paid', and there is no
further tax to pay by the investment trust. Unfranked income
includes income from all untaxed sources – for example,
foreign share dividends, interest and underwriting
commission, and is taxable in the trust's hands.

Fully invested
If all the money in a trust is invested, rather than having
some held in cash form, the trust is said to be fully invested.

Gearing
Also known, particularly in the US, as leverage. Gearing is
the process whereby capital growth and income to the
ordinary shareholders of a trust are boosted by borrowings,
which provide scope for additional investment but which carry
a fixed liability. The return on this extra investment minus
the costs of borrowing the money gives the shareholder an
enhanced or geared profit.

Gearing factor
Gearing is expressed in the AITC's monthly information service
as the amount by which the net asset value per share would
grow if the trust's assets invested in equities were to double
in value. This is the gearing feactor.

General/generalist trust
A trust with a wide spread of investments and objectives
which include provision of income as well as capital growth.

Geographical spread
The way in which investments in a portfolio are distributed

over different world markets. The geographical spread of a trust might be, for instance, 40% UK, 20% US, 20% Japan and 20% Europe.

Going-concern basis
The method of calculating a company's net asset value where prior charges are deducted at their market value. The alternative method is known as a break-up basis, and is the more conservative of the two (see Break-up basis; Prior charges).

Gross
Without deductions. A gross dividend is a dividend percentage expressed without deduction of tax.

Hedging
The process of cutting the currency exposure of a trust portfolio, and hence reducing the effect of exchange rate fluctuations on the portfolio's value. This is achieved by the use of financial futures contracts, foreign currency loans, or other instruments.

Income shares
In a dual capital trust, the class of shares which is entitled to receive all the trust's income.

Independent investment trust
A trust which has its own team of managers, rather than hiring the services of an outside management group.

Institutional investor
An institutional investor, as opposed to a private investor, is a large City organisation such as an insurance company, a pension fund manager or a bank. An investment trust itself is also an institutional investor. Institutional investors deal in very large amounts and often build up sizeable shareholdings. This means they have a good deal of power in influencing the way the company they have invested in is run and deciding its fate in the event of a takeover bid.

Interim (see Dividend)

148

Investment trust company
A company which exists to invest its shareholders' capital in a range of financial assets, mostly quoted companies, and to obtain the best possible return in terms of capital growth and dividend. Shares in investment trust companies quoted on the London stock market are bought and sold in the same way as ICI or Marks & Spencer. Their price varies according to supply and demand, as well as other factors, including changes in the trust's net asset value, though most trusts trade at a discount to net asset value. As the amount of capital in issue does not fluctuate with investor demand, investment trusts in other countries are sometimes described as 'closed-end funds'.

Leverage (see Gearing)

Limited life trust
A trust which has a fixed date by which it must be wound up.

Liquidity
The amount within a portfolio which is held in cash rather than being invested.

Liquidation
The process of terminating a company by realising its assets, paying off creditors and holders of loan capital, and distributing the remaining assets among shareholders, according to the correct order of priority.

Listed investments
Investments which have an official listing on one of the world's recognised stock markets. Also known as quoted investments.

Loan stock
This pays holders a fixed rate of interest and is repayable on or by a given date. Loan Stocks are usually unsecured. (See Debenture stock).

Management buyout
A process whereby the managers of a company become its owners by buying it out from the existing owner or parent company. Also known in the US as a leveraged buyout, because part of the purchase price is financed by short-term load capital provided by institutions.

Management charge
The annual charge made by the managers of an investment trust for their services. More loosely, the amount of total management expenses appearing in the accounts, including general expenses, directors' emoluments and audit fees.

Management company
A company which manages investment trusts.

Management group
A group of investment trusts which are managed jointly, with the management company which actually runs the trust portfolios sometimes being a wholly-owned group subsidiary.

Market capitalisation
The value of a company as determined by multiplying the number of shares in issue by the price of the shares.

Market price
There are two prices quoted by dealers. The higher or offer price at which they will sell you shares and the lower or bid price at which they will buy your shares. The difference between the two is known as the 'spread' or 'turn'. (See Mid-market price.)

Market value
The value of a shareholding, calculated by multiplying the number of shares held by the mid-market price or, more rarely, by the bid price of the share.

Marketability
The ease or otherwise with which shares in a specific company can be bought or sold. If a company has 'poor marketability', it means that not many shares are in circulation, and that both buying and selling may be difficult. Poor marketability is obviously a problem when you come to sell shares. The fact that there are few people who want to buy will mean that the price offered may be very low or it may not be possible to sell at all. Marketability is not likely to prove a problem for the private investment trust shareholder, who deals in relatively small quantities of shares, but it may be for an institution which wants to dispose of a large investment trust holding.

Mid-market price
A price between the offer and bid prices at which shares are bought and sold. The mid-market price is used to calculate investment trust performance statistics. It is also the price used in most newspaper share tables.

Net
After deductions. A net dividend is quoted after deduction of tax (see also Net asset value).

Net asset value (NAV)
The net asset value of an investment trust is the value of the assets after deduction of all prior charges, and is usually expressed in pence per share. Net asset value total return as shown in the AITC monthly figures is the growth in net asset value, assuming that incoming dividends are reinvested in the trust's underlying assets. (See Reinvestment of dividends.)

Nominal value
The nominal value of a loan stock is the face value, or value at which it will eventually be redeemed, and is also described as the par value or the redemption value. The nominal value of a share is shown in a company's memorandum of association.

Offer price
The price at which you buy shares, and the higher of the two share prices quoted.

Options
Technically, options are a different type of financial instrument from warrants, but more loosely the two terms are used as if they were interchangeable (see Warrants).

Ordinary shares
The main type of equity capital, and the main sort of investment trust share which is of interest to the private investor (see Equity capital).

Over-the-counter market
In some countries the over-the-counter market provides an informal dealing mechanism in the shares of companies which

151

may be too small to have an official stock market quotation. Over-the-counter (OTC) shares may be riskier than the average.

Overweight/underweight
A portfolio is said to be overweight or underweight in a particular world market if its holding in that market represents a higher or lower percentage of its total portfolio than the capitalisation of the market concerned as a percentage of total world market capitalisation. In other words, if the Japanese market represents 25% of the world total, and a certain trust has 30% of its portfolio invested in the Japanese market, it is overweight in Japan. Basic sector weightings are calculated by reference to the percentage each sector accounts for in the total market index. If a trust's holdings in a particular sector are less than that sector's percentage of the index, the trust is underweight in that sector.

PEPs
PEPs, or Personal Equity Plans, were first available on 1 January 1987. UK taxpayers over eighteen can invest up to £6,000 (1990/91) in a PEPs, and the investment must be in UK quoted shares, though 50% can be in a qualifying investment trust. The proceeds are free of capital gains tax and dividends received are not subject to income tax.

Par value (see Nominal value)

Participation (see Equity participation)

Portfolio
A collection of investments held by a single investor, whether an investment trust or an individual. A portfolio may be the total investments held by the investor, or all the investments of one type. For instance, one might talk about the unlisted portfolio, the UK portfolio or the European portfolio of an investment trust.

P.P.S.
Pence per share.

Preference shares
A class of share capital which receives a fixed rate of return, and comes ahead of ordinary shares in the order of priority in a winding-up (see Cumulative; Equity capital).

Premium
If the share price of an investment trust is higher than the net asset value, the trust is said to stand at a premium. The premium is shown as a percentage of the share price. It is rare for an investment trust to be at a premium (see Discount).

Prior charges
A trust's fixed liabilities, including all types of loan capital, and usually preference shares. Prior charges are deducted from the trust's total assets to give the net asset value. There are two different ways of expressing prior charges for the net asset value calculation: at the par value, or the value at which charges would have to be redeemed, or at the market value, that is, the value the charges currently have in the market. Taking prior charges at their market value ('at market') is the less conservative way of doing the calculation; taking them 'at par' (or at nominal or redemption value) is the more conservative calculation.

Prospectus
The document which describes a company to prospective shareholders when its shares are first issued.

Quoted investments (see Listed investments)

Recovery situations
Companies which have been through a difficult period, but which are expected to have a brighter future, whether because of a change in relevant market conditions, management restructuring, or other reasons.

Redemption value (see Par value)

Reinvestment of dividends
For purposes of 'total return' performance statistics, it is assumed that any dividend received on an investment trust company share is used to buy more of the trust's shares. For the individual investor, it has been difficult in practice to

reinvest dividends until recently, when trusts with regular savings schemes have begun to offer this facility.

Report and accounts
The annual document in which the directors of the company report the company's results for the past year, give the accounts for the year, and comment on any relevant matters.

Rights issue
A new issue of shares whereby existing shareholders are offered one or more new shares for every share they hold, at a fixed price which is lower than the market price.

Scrip issue (see Bonus issue)

Secondary markets
Stock markets which do not have the full status of a country's main stock exchange. They are set up to allow smaller companies to apply for a listing, making their shares more marketable. The UK Unlisted Securities Market and the French Second Marché are examples of secondary markets.

Share listing
The process of getting a company's shares listed, or quoted, on the stock market, so that they can be freely bought and sold in a properly regulated way.

Share price total return
In the AITC's performance figures, the share price return including reinvestment of dividends in additional shares at their market price (see Reinvestment of dividends).

Special situations
Companies where there is an unusual set of circumstances affecting future prospects. Some trusts have a portfolio emphasis on special situations, which may include recovery stocks, management buyouts, or companies which are expected to be takeover prospects.

Specialist trusts
Trusts whose portfolios are limited to a relatively narrow range of investments – Japanese shares, smaller companies shares, or commodity shares, for instance. Specialist trusts

154

usually invest mainly for growth rather than income, and tend to be more volatile than general trusts.

Split capital trust (see Dual capital trust)

Stepped interest debenture stock (STUD)
A debenture on which the rate of interest payable by the trust starts relatively low and builds up over the life of the stock.

Stock market index
An average share price movement based on a number of companies from an individual stock market. This is used as a guide to the performance of the market as a whole. In the UK, the best known indices are the Financial Times Actuaries All Share Index (the FTA All Share), the Financial Times Industrial Ordinary Share Index (the FT Ordinary or 30-Share Index), and the Financial Times Stock Exchange 100 Index (the FTSE 100 or 'Footsie'). There is a special index for the investment trust sector: the Financial Times Actuaries Investment Trust Index. Other widely used world indices are: the Dow Jones Industrial and the Standard and Poors Composite (USA); the Tokyo New Stock Exchange (Japan); the Hang Seng Index (Hong Kong); the Frankfurt Commerzbank Index (Germany) and the Morgan Stanley Capital International World Index (Worldwide).

Total return (see Net asset value; Share price total return)

Underweight (see Overweight)

Underwriting commission
The fee paid to an investment trust or other City institution for guaranteeing to 'underwrite' an issue of new shares that is, to buy any shares which may remain unsold. The fee is paid whether or not the trust has to make any purchases.

Unfranked income (see Franked income)

Unit trust
A managed pool of investors' funds constituted as a trust, with a trustee who is separate from the fund managers. The fund is not closed-end, like an investment trust, because units

can be created or liquidated as necessary, depending on demand. Units are bought from the managers, and the unit price is calculated from the basis of net asset value, with costs being added or subtracted to give an offer or bid price. There are over 1,000 unit trusts.

Unitisation
The process of turning an investment trust into a unit trust by 'unitising' the shares.

Unlisted investments
Investments in companies which have no stock market listing. Also called unquoted investments.

Unquoted investments (see Unlisted investments)

Unsecured loan stock (see Loan stock)

Venture capital
The business of making high risk investments in small and young companies, often with a high technology bias, which may already be trading, or may be at the planning stage.

Warrants
Also described sometimes as options. These are contracts which permit the holder to buy the associated ordinary share at a specified price within a certain period of time.

Weighting (see Overweight/underweight)

Winding-up (see Liquidation)

Yield
The yield on an investment trust (or any other share) indicates the size of the income return on the share in relation to the price you have to pay for it. It is calculated by dividing the annual gross dividend into the current share price.

DIRECTORY OF
STOCKBROKING SERVICES

ABERDEEN

Allied Provincial Securities Ltd
Parsons Penney & Co
25 Albyn Place
ABERDEEN   AB1 1YL
Tel: 0224 589345
Contact: Mr Hutton
(IT PEP available)

AYLESBURY

Broker Financial Services plc
Friars Court
Friarage Passage
AYLESBURY   HP20 2SJ
Tel: 0296 399633
Contact: James Greener
(Portfolio Mgt & PEPs)
(IFA: IMRO Member)

BATH

Godfray Derby & Co
(Division of National Investment
Group)
1 Northumberland Buildings
BATH   BA1 2JB
Tel: 0225 337100
Fax: 0225 314281
Contact: Neil Dowdney

Allied Provincial Securities Ltd
Laws & Co
38 Gay Street
BATH   BA1 2NT
Tel: 0225 335616
Contact: Simon Halliday
(IT PEP available)

BELFAST

BWD Rensburg Ltd
St George's House
99-101 High Street
BELFAST   BT1 2AH
Tel: 0232 321002
Contact: W Gavin Graham

Josias Cunningham & Co
2 Bridge Street
BELFAST
BT1 1NX
Tel: 0232 246005
Contact: H R Herron

BIRMINGHAM

Chambers and Remington Ltd
Canterbury House
85 Newhall Street
BIRMINGHAM   B3 1LS
Tel: 021 236 2577
Contact: Mrs C Wilkinson

Harris Allday Lea & Brooks
33 Great Charles Street
BIRMINGHAM   B3 3JN
Tel: 021 233 1222
Contact: R Treverton Jones

Allied Provincial Securities Ltd
Murray & Co
Beaufort House
94-96 Newhall Street
BIRMINGHAM   B3 1PE
Tel: 021 200 3377
Contact: Mr J P Cadwallader
(IT PEP available)

157

Smith Keen Cutler
Exchange Buildings
Stephenson Place
BIRMINGHAM   B2 4NN
Tel: 021 643 9977
Contact: Philip A Cropper

Stock Beech & Co
Beech House
Greenfield Crescent
Edgbaston
BIRMINGHAM   B15 3BB
Tel: 021 451 1818
Contact: Tim Abrahams

BLACKPOOL

James Brearley & Sons
56-58 Caunce Street
BLACKPOOL   FY1 3DQ
Tel: 0253 28686
Contact: David Battersby

BOURNEMOUTH

Parrish Stockbrokers
3 Poole Road
BOURNEMOUTH
Dorset   BH2 5QJ
Tel: 0202 297331
Contact: Michael Prince

Robson Cotterell Limited
Bourne Chambers
St Peters Road
BOURNEMOUTH   BH1 2JX
Tel: 0202 27581
Contact: A R Oliver

BRADFORD

BWD Rensburg Ltd
Broadway House
9 Bank Street
BRADFORD   BD1 1HJ
Tel: 0274 729406
Contact: Andrew Goodchild

BRIDGNORTH

Harris Allday Lea & Brooks
2 St Leonard's Close
BRIDGNORTH
Shropshire
Tel: 0746 761444
Contact: A J Whitehead

BRISTOL

Bristol and London Financial
  Management
29 Great George Street
BRISTOL   BS1 5QT
Tel: 0272 253325
Contact: Marcel Carrier
(IFA: FIMBRA Member)

Greig Middleton & Co Ltd
Court House
Tailor's Court
Broad Street
BRISTOL   BS1 2EX
Tel: 0272 264013
Contact: Martin Bishop

Hargreaves Lansdown Asset
Management Limited
Embassy House, Queen's Avenue
Clifton
BRISTOL   BS8 1SB
Tel: 0272 741309
Contact: Charles Carlyle
(IFA: FIMBRA Member)

Allied Provincial Securities Ltd
Laws & Co
40 Queen Square
BRISTOL   BS1 4DU
Tel: 0272 293901
(IT PEP available)

Stock Beech & Co
Spectrum
Bond Street
BRISTOL   BS1 3DE
Tel: 0272 20051
Contact: James Fox

Whitechurch Securities
36 Westbury Lane
BRISTOL   BS9 2PP
Tel: 0272 687277
Contact: Kean Seager
(IFA: FIMBRA Member)

CAMBRIDGE

Charles Stanley & Co Ltd
9 Pembroke Street
CAMBRIDGE   CB2 3QY
Tel: 0223 316726
Contact: Chris Day

CARDIFF

Allied Provincial Securities Ltd
Westgate House
Womanby Street
CARDIFF   CF1 2UD
Tel: 0222 397672
Contact: D Cantlay
(IT PEP available)

Bell Lawrie White & Co Ltd
Sutherland House
Castlebridge
Cowbridge Road East
CARDIFF   DF1 9AB
Tel: 0222 340100

CARLISLE

Allied Provincial Securities Ltd
1 Cecil Street
CARLISLE   CA1 1NL
Tel: 0228 21200
Contact: Tony Lamb
(IT PEP available)

CHELTENHAM

Bell Lawrie White & Co Ltd
Investment Trust Mgt Services
Harley House
29 Cambray Place
CHELTENHAM   GL50 1JN
Tel: 0242 577677
Contact: Paul Nurden

CHICHESTER

Cobbold Roach Ltd
2 Newtown
East Pallant
CHICHESTER
West Sussex   PO19 1UG
Tel: 0243 775373
Contact: D Edwards

CIRENCESTER

Parrish Stockbrokers
The Old Coach House
Dyer Street
CIRENCESTER   GL7 2PF
Tel: 0285 650101
Contact: Roger Swift

COLCHESTER

Parrish Stockbrokers
76 East Hill
COLCHESTER   CO1 2QN
Tel: 0206 869992
Contact: G L W Burlton

COLWYN BAY

Allied Provincial Securities Ltd
15 Wynnstay Road
COLWYN BAY   LL29 8NN
Tel: 0492 530354
Contact: John Waring
(IT PEP available)

COVENTRY

Credit Suisse Buckmaster &
  Moore
30 Warwick Row
COVENTRY   CV1 1EY
Tel: 0203 632323
Contact: Tony Huntington

DUNDEE

Allied Provincial Securities Ltd
Parsons Penney & Co
PO Box 84
41 North Lindsay Street
DUNDEE   DD1 1PW
Tel: 0382 21081
Contact: Ms A Doughty
(IT PEP available)

EDINBURGH

Allied Provincial Securities Ltd
Parsons Penney & Co
12 Melville Crescent
EDINBURGH   EH3 7LU
Tel: 031 226 4466
Contact: Angus Tod
(IT PEP available)

Bell Lawrie White & Co Ltd
Investment Trust Mgt Service
Norloch House
36 King's Stables Road
EDINBURGH   EH1 2EU
Tel: 031 228 5777
Contact: Edwin Lilley/Ann Brint

Castle Cairn Fund Managers Ltd
Cairn House
61 Dublin Street
EDINBURGH   EH3 6NL
Tel: 031 557 6868
Contact: Simon C Murphy
(IFA: IMRO member)

EXETER

Allied Provincial Securities Ltd
Westlake & Co
Broadwalk House
Southernhay West
EXETER   EX1 1TS
Tel: 0392 410277
Contact: Mr P Hewson
(IT PEP available)

FAREHAM

Hilliard Wallace & Partners
Lothian House
22 High Street
FAREHAM
Hants   PO16 7AE
Tel: 0329 288641
Contact: Keith Field
(IFA: FIMBRA Member)

Lawrence Clarke & Partners
(Representative of the Burns
Anderson Independent Network)
1st Floor Suite
Riverside House
Upper Wharf
FAREHAM
Hampshire   PO16 0LZ
Tel: 0329 236231
Contact: Larry Clarke
(IFA: FIMBRA C1 Member)

FARNHAM

W I Carr (Investments) Ltd
Clock House
Dogflud Way
FARNHAM
Surrey   GU9 7UD
Tel: 0252 733345
Contact: D Aldrich-Blake

GLASGOW

BWD Rensburg Ltd
48 West Regent Street
GLASGOW   G2 2RB
Tel: 041 333 9323
Contact: Alistair Cumming

Campbell Neill & Co Ltd
Stock Exchange House
7 Nelson Mandela Place
GLASGOW   G2 1JN
Tel: 041 248 6271
Contact: E Duckett

Greig Middleton & Co Ltd
Pacific House
70 Wellington Street
GLASGOW   G2 6UD
Tel: 041 221 8103
Contact: Mark Sherriff

Allied Provincial Securities Ltd
Parsons Penney & Co
155 St Vincent Street
GLASGOW   G2 5NN
Tel: 041 204 1886
Contact: Mrs S D Biggart

Speirs & Jeffrey Ltd
36 Renfield Street
GLASGOW   G2 1NE
Tel: 041 248 4311
Contact: Peter C M Roger

GUILDFORD

Greig Middleton & Co Ltd
Highgate House
214 High Street
GUILDFORD
Surrey   GU1 3JX
Tel: 0483 300585
Contact: Jocelyn Penn-Bull

HARROGATE

Cawood, Smithie & Co
22 East Parade
HARROGATE   HG1 5LT
Tel: 0423 530035
Contact: Stephen Jackson

Redmayne-Bentley
c/o Dillon's, The Book Store
40 James Street
HARROGATE   HG1 1RF
Tel: 0423 526886
Contact: P H Meyrick

HARTLEPOOL

Cawood, Smithie & Co
73 Church Street
HARTLEPOOL
Cleveland   TS24 7DN
Tel: 0429 272231
Contact: Don Welsh

HEREFORD

Greenwell Montagu Stockbrokers
35 Bridge Street
HEREFORD
HR4 9DG
Tel: 0432 264646
Contact: John Entwisle/
    Clive Loader/Sue Holden

HUDDERSFIELD

BWD Rensburg Ltd
Woodsome House
Woodsome Park, Fenay Bridge
HUDDERSFIELD   HD8 0JG
Tel: 0484 608066
Contact: Simon G Kaye

INVERNESS

Campbell Neill & Co Ltd
Ballantyne House
84 Academy Street
INVERNESS   IV1 1LU
Tel: 0463 223773
Contact: John Mulhern

IPSWICH

Charles Stanley & Co Ltd
16 Northgate Street
IPSWICH   IP1 3DB
Tel: 0473 210264
Contact: Mr B M Marshall

LEAMINGTON SPA

RIM Fund Management Ltd
Vivian House
21 Market Hill
SOUTHAM
Warwickshire   CV33 0HF
Tel: 0926 814552
Contact: Simon Russell
(IFA: FIMBRA Member)

LEEDS

Allied Provincial Securities Ltd
Town Centre House
The Merrion Centre
LEEDS   LS2 8NA
Tel: 0532 420303
Contact: Mr E Pollicott
(IT PEP available)

BWD Rensburg Ltd
3 Park Court
Park Cross Street
LEEDS   LS1 2QH
Tel: 0532 434631
Contact: Simon M Fiather

Redmayne-Bentley
Merton House
84 Albion Street
LEEDS   LS1 6AG
Tel: 0532 436941
Contact: J A W Collins

LEICESTER

Wilshere Baldwin & Co
19 The Crescent
King Street
LEICESTER   LE1 6RX
Tel: 0533 541344
Contact: M J Cufflin

LIVERPOOL

BWD Rensburg Ltd
Silkhouse Court
Tithebarn Street
LIVERPOOL   L2 2NH
Tel: 051 227 2030
Contact: Martin Cooke

Charterhouse Tilney
385 Sefton House
Exchange Building
LIVERPOOL   L2 3RT
Tel: 051 236 6000
Contact: J D Mitchell

LLANDUDNO

Henry Cooke Lumsden plc
59 Madoc Street
LLANDUDNO   LL30 2TW
Tel: 0492 74391
Contact: Craig Towler

LONDON

Allied Provincial Securities Ltd
Shackleton House
4 Battlebridge Lane
LONDON   SE1 2HY
Tel: 071 378 0015
Contact: Mr G Brackenbridge
(IT PEP available)

Brewin Dolphin & Co Ltd
5 Giltspur Street
LONDON
EC1A 8DE
Tel: 071 248 4400
Contact: Mark Bareham

CL-Alexanders Laing &
 Cruickshank
Piercy House
7 Copthall Avenue
LONDON   EC2R 7BE
Tel: 071 588 2800

Cobbold Roach Ltd
Greenly House
40 Dukes Place
LONDON   EC3A 5PX
Tel: 071 782 0066
Contact: Derek Keen

Henry Cooke Lumsden plc
Crowne House
56/58 Southwark Street
LONDON   SE1 1UL
Tel: 071 378 1717
Contact: David Lumsden

Credit-Suisse Buckmaster &
 Moore Ltd
80 Cannon Street
LONDON   EC4N 6HH
Tel: 071 588 2868
Contact: George Lynne

Dunbar Boyle & Kingsley Ltd
Astral House
125/129 Middlesex Street
LONDON   E1 7JF
Tel: 071 623 9898
Contact: Robin Boyle

Granville Davies Ltd
8 Lovat Lane
LONDON
EC3R 8BP
Tel: 071 621 1212
Contact: David King

Greenwell Montagu Stockbrokers
114 Old Broad Street
LONDON
EC2P 2HY
Tel: 071 588 8817
Contact: Tim Wakeley
Managing Director

Greig Middleton & Co Ltd
66 Wilson Street
LONDON
EC2A 2BL
Tel: 071 247 0007
Contact: Michael Read/
David Thomas

GH & AM Jay
61 Cheapside
LONDON
EC2 6AX
Tel: 071 248 0081

Keith Bayley Rogers & Co
194-200 Bishopsgate
LONDON
EC2N 4NR
Tel: 071 623 2400
Contact: Michael Dodd

Killik & Co
45 Cadogan Street
LONDON   SW3 2QJ
Tel: 071 589 1577
Contact: P G Killik

Kleinwort Benson Investment
 Management Ltd
10 Fenchurch Street
LONDON   EC3M 3LB
Tel: 071 623 8000
Contact: David Chappel
(IFA: IMRO Member)

Laurence Keen & Co
49/51 Bow Lane
Cheapside
LONDON   EC4M 9LX
Tel: 071 489 9493
Contact: M Reid Scott

Olliff & Partners plc
Saddlers House
Gutter Lane
Cheapside
LONDON
EC2V 6BR
Tel: 071 374 0191
Contact: Lorraine Goodhew

Pilling & Company
1 Roscoe Street
LONDON   EC1Y 8JP
Tel: 071 253 8111
Contact: S C P Chittenden

Quilter Goodison Company Ltd
Garrard House
31-45 Gresham Street
LONDON   EC2V 7LH
Tel: 071 600 4177
Contact: Sir William Goring

Sheppards
1 London Bridge
LONDON   SE1 9QU
Tel: 071 378 7000
Contact: J M Cobb

Charles Stanley & Co Ltd
18 Finsbury Circus
LONDON   EC2M 7BL
Tel: 071 638 5717
Contact: Brian Goodhall

Svenska & Company Limited
Svenska House
3-5 Newgate Street
LONDON   EC1A 7DA
Tel: 071 329 4484
Contact: A J Cresswell

Taylor Young Investment
 Management Limited
45 Curlew Street
Butlers Wharf
LONDON   SE1 2ND
Tel: 071 407 3452
Contacts: David Fisher/
Christopher Taylor-Young
(discretionary basis only)
(IFA: IMRO Member)

Touche Remnant & Co
Investment Trust Management
 Service
Mermaid House
2 Puddle Dock
LONDON   EC4V 3AT
Tel: 071 236 6565
Contact: Roddy Maclean
(Minimum investment: £20,000)
(IFA: IMRO Member)

Vivian Gray & Co
Ling House
10-13 Dominion Street
LONDON   EC2M 2UX
Tel: 071 638 2888
Contact: W G Harris

Walker, Crips, Weddle,
 Beck & Co plc
Kemp House
152-160 City Road
LONDON   EC1Y 2PQ
Tel: 071 253 7502
Contact: Mr Field

LYMINGTON

Greenwell Montagu Stockbrokers
98 High Street
Lymington
HANTS   SO41 9AP
Tel: 0590 74288
Contact: Sebastian Chamberlain

MANCHESTER

Bell Lawrie White & Co Ltd
Investment Trust Mgt Service
3rd Floor
Brazennose House
Brazennose Street
MANCHESTER   M2 5BP
Tel: 061 832 9979
Contact: Bill Thomson

Henry Cooke Lumsden plc
PO Box 369
1 King Street
MANCHESTER   M60 3AH
Tel: 061 834 2332
Contact: James Bardner

Allied Provincial Securities Ltd
Illingworth Henriques & Co
Ashworth Sons & Barratt
St James Court
30 Brown Street
MANCHESTER   M60 2JE
Tel: 061 832 4812
Contact: Mr K Tucker
(IT PEP available)

Pilling & Company
12 St Ann's Square
MANCHESTER   M2 7HT
Tel: 061 832 6581
Contact: David A Nugent

John Siddall & Son Ltd
The Stock Exchange
PO Box 499
4 Norfolk Street
MANCHESTER   M60 1DY
Tel: 061 835 3130
Contact: K McKenna

MIDDLESBROUGH

Cawood, Smithie & Co
48a High Street
Stockesley
MIDDLESBROUGH   TS9 5AX
Tel: 0642 712771
Contact: Arthur Harris

Allied Provincial Securities Ltd
Stancliffe & Co
City House
206-208 Marton Road
MIDDLESBROUGH   TS4 2JE
Tel: 0642 249211
Contact: Mr J Taylor
(IT PEP available)

NEWCASTLE UPON TYNE

Coleman Lovell
20 Leazes Park Road
NEWCASTLE UPON TYNE
NE1 4PG
Contact: Barnett Alexander
(Warrants specialist)

Wise Speke Ltd
Commercial Union House
39 Pilgrim Street
NEWCASTLE UPON TYNE
NE1
Tel: 091 2611266
Contact: N T Garbutt

Allied Provincial Securities Ltd
John S Smith & Co
Central Exchange Buildings
128 Grainger Street
NEWCASTLE UPON TYNE
NE1 5AF
Tel: 091 232 6695
Contact: Mr D Bewick
(IT PEP available)

NEWPORT, ISLE OF WIGHT

Cobbold Roach Ltd
35 Orchard Street
NEWPORT
Isle of Wight   PO30 1JZ
Tel: 0983 520922
Contact: P Coke

NORWICH

Barclays Bank Trust Company Ltd
East Anglia Regional Office
Lawrence House
St Andrews Hill
NORWICH   NR2 1HQ
Tel: 0603 660255
Contact: Godfrey Smith

Barratt & Cooke
5 Opie Street
NORWICH   NR1 3DW
Tel: 0603 624236/7
Contact C W L Barratt

Charles Stanley & Co Ltd
24 Castle Meadow
NORWICH   NR1 3DH
Tel: 0603 665990
Contact: Willy Brownlow

NOTTINGHAM

Allied Provincial Securities Ltd
William Chapman, Trease & Co
Norwich Union House
South Parade
NOTTINGHAM   NG1 2LN
Tel: 0602 476772
Contact: Mrs Hibbert
(IT PEP available)

PERTH

Campbell Neill & Co Ltd
63 Tay Street
PERTH   PH2 8NN
Tel: 0738 37441
Contact: Douglas Gibson

PETERBOROUGH

Allied Provincial Securities Ltd
Trinity Court
Trinity Street
PETERBOROUGH   PE1 1DA
Tel: 0733 555131
Contact: Mr P Organ
(IT PEP available)

PLYMOUTH

Allied Provincial Securities Ltd
Westlake & Co
St Catherine's House
Notte Street
PLYMOUTH   PL1 2TW
Tel: 0752 220971
Contact: Mr M Manisty
(IT PEP available)

RAMSEY (ISLE OF MAN)

Allied Provincial Securities Ltd
Illingworth Henriques & Co
PO Chambers
2 Court Row
RAMSEY ISLE OF MAN
Tel: 0624 812925
Contact: Mr R Bellwood
(IT PEP available)

REDRUTH

Allied Provincial Securities Ltd
Westlake & Co
27A Fore Street
REDRUTH   TR15 2BQ
Tel: 0209 214488
Contact: Mr G Roland
(IT PEP available)

SALISBURY

Cobbold Roach Ltd
43/55 Milford Street
SALISBURY
Wilts   SP1 2BP
Tel: 0722 330333
Contact: B Gore-Brown

SHEFFIELD

Allied Provincial Securities Ltd
Omega Court
Cemetery Road
SHEFFIELD   S11 8FT
Tel: 0742 684 298
Contact: Mr C Redman
(IT PEP available)

BWD Rensburg Ltd
Wharncliffe House
Bank Street
SHEFFIELD   S1 2DS
Tel: 0742 722292
Contact: Nigel G Bates

SOUTHAMPTON

Branston & Gothard Ltd
Ground Floor
Prudential Buildings, Above Bar
SOUTHAMPTON   SO1 0FG
Tel: 0703 229229
Contact: P Simou, FinstD,MBIM,TCA

Cobbold Roach Ltd
The Director-General's House
Rockstone Place
The Avenue
SOUTHAMPTON   SO9 1XL
Tel: 0703 330130
Contact: T Bell

STIRLING

Campbell Neill & Co Ltd
18 Maxwell Place
STIRLING   FK8 1JU
Tel: 0786 73817
Contact: Michael Stewart

STOKE ON TRENT

P H Pope & Son
6 Pall Mall
Hanley
STOKE ON TRENT   ST1 1EU
Tel: 0782 202154

SWINDON

Brewin Dolphin & Co Ltd
Anglia House
115/118 Commercial Road
SWINDON
Wilts   SN1 5PL
Tel: 0793 616001
Contact: A R Irvine-Fortescue

TAUNTON

Cobbold Roach Ltd
4 Chartfield House
Castle Street
TAUNTON
Somerset   TA1 4AS
Tel: 0823 259711
Contact: P A C Moore/
 Robert Doughton

TIVERTON

Cobbold Roach Ltd
The Clockhouse
East Anstey
TIVERTON   EX16 9JB
Tel: 03984 329
Contact: D Beall

Trumark Financial Services Ltd
8 Angel Hill
TIVERTON
Devon   EX16 6PE
Tel: 0884 253850/258980

TORQUAY

Allied Provincial Securities Ltd
Westlake & Co
Provincial House
1 Strand
TORQUAY   TQ1 2RH
Tel: 0803 297337
Contact: Mr M Clapham
(IT PEP available)

TRURO

Greig Middleton & Co Ltd
Eagle Star House
Lemon Street
TRURO   TR1 2PX
Tel: 0872 222485
Contact: Jeremy Sharp

TUNBRIDGE WELLS

Cawood, Smithie & Co
Lonsdale House
7 Lonsdale Gardens
TUNBRIDGE WELLS
Kent   TN1 1NU
Tel: 0642 515840
Contact: Bill Day

Cobbold Roach Ltd
5 York Road
TUNBRIDGE WELLS
Kent   TN1 1JX
Tel: 0892 515156
Contact: R C Corfield

WARWICK

RIM Fund Management Ltd
Vivian House
21 Market Hill
SOUTHAM
Warwickshire   CV33 0HF
Tel: 092681 4552
Contact: Simon Russell
(IFA: FIMBRA Member)

WESTON SUPER MARE

Allied Provincial Securities Ltd
Laws & Co
115 High Street
WESTON SUPER MARE
Avon   BS22 1HQ
Tel: 0934 413355
Contact: Mr J Scott
(IT PEP available)

WINCHESTER

Cobbold Roach Ltd
Calpe House
St Thomas Street
WINCHESTER   SO23 8BJ
Tel: 0962 52362
Contact: Graham Wells

YORK

Greig Middleton & Co Ltd
23 High Petergate
YORK   YO1 2HS
Tel: 0904 647911
Contact: David Pearson

FIMBRA = Financial Intermediaries, Managers and
Brokers Regulatory Association

IMRO = Investment Management Regulatory
Organisation

We trust that the information contained herein is
accurate. If you know of any corrections, however,
please let us know. In addition, if you would like to
draw our attention to an independent financial adviser/
stockbroker who you believe should be placed on this
list, please write to:

Eleanor Burton, Information Officer, AITC, Park House
(6th Floor), 16 Finsbury Circus, London EC2M 7JJ

Source: AITC (1991)

Investment Trusts

ABERDEEN FUND MANAGERS LTD
10 Queens Terrace, Aberdeen, AB9 1QJ
Telephone 0224 631999
Contact: Atholl Forbes

Investment Trusts
Abtrust New Dawn
Abtrust New European
Abtrust New Thai

ALLIANCE TRUST PLC
SECOND ALLIANCE TRUST PLC
Meadow House, Reform Street, Dundee DD1 1TJ
Telephone 0382 201700
Contact: Gavin Suggett

ARGOSY ASSET MANAGEMENT PLC
30 Finsbury Circus, London EC2M 7QQ
Telephone 071 588 6000
Contact: A J Prigent

Investment Trusts
Clydesdale
Ensign
New Frontiers Development
Turkey
Worth

BAILLIE GIFFORD & CO
10 Glenfinlas Street, Edinburgh EH3 6YY
Telephone 031 225 2581
Contact: Michael Usher

Investment Trusts
Baillie Gifford Japan   Monks
Baillie Gifford Shin Nippon   Scottish Mortgage
Baillie Gifford Technology
Mid Wynd International

BARING PRIVATE INVESTMENT
MANAGEMENT LIMITED
155 Bishopsgate, London EC2M 3XY
Telephone 071 628 6000
Contact: R E Little

Investment Trusts
Stratton
Tribune

BERKELEY GOVETT
INTERNATIONAL LIMITED
Minden House, 6 Minden Place, St Helier,
Jersey JE2 4WQ
Telephone 0534 38578
Contact: Mr C Chaplin

Investment Trusts
Govett American Endeavour

BERKELEY PHOENIX MANAGEMENT LTD
Wellington House, Union Street, St Helier, Jersey
Telephone 0534 58847
Contact: Peter Scott Graham

Investment Trusts
Jersey Phoenix

BERMUDA INTERNATIONAL
SECURITIES LIMITED
2 Broadgate, London EC2M 7ED
Telephone 071 256 4000
Contact: Andrew Green

Investment Trusts
Siam Selective Growth Trust plc

BETA FUNDS LIMITED
60 Borough High Street, London SE1 1XF
Telephone 071 407 6610
Contact: Carmen Hakham

Investment Trusts
Beta Global Emerging Markets

BROWN SHIPLEY ASSET MANAGEMENT

Founders Court, Lothbury, London EC2
Telephone 071 606 9833
Contact: W Stuttaford
Investment Trusts
New Guernsey Securities

CS INVESTMENT MANAGEMENT LTD

125 High Holborn, London WC1V 6PY
Telephone 071 242 1148
Contact: Frank Smith
Investment Trusts
Group Development Capital

CANDOVER INVESTMENTS PLC

20 Old Bailey, London EC4M 7LN
Telephone 071 489 9848
Contact: C R E Brooke

CAPITAL GEARING TRUST PLC

34 Upper Queen Street, Belfast BT1 6HG
Telephone 0232 244001
Contact: Blanche Watt

CAPITAL HOUSE INVESTMENT MANAGEMENT LIMITED

6 New Bridge Street, London EC4V 6JH
Telephone 071 353 5050
Contact: Jenny Prince
Investment Trusts
London & New York Convertible

CASTLE CAIRN FUND MANAGERS LTD

Cairn House, 61 Dublin Street, Edinburgh EH3 6NL
Telephone 031 557 6868
Contact: Simon Murphy
Investment Trusts
Castle Cairn

CAZENOVE & CO

12 Tokenhouse Yard, London EC2R 7AN
Telephone 071 588 2828
Contact: Graham Venn
Investment Trusts
Hotspur Investments

DISCRETIONARY UNIT FUND MANAGERS LIMITED

66 Wilson Street, London EC2A 2BL
Telephone 071 377 8819
Contact: S Knott
Investment Trusts
Rights & Issues

DUNEDIN FUND MANAGERS LTD

25 Ravelston Terrace, Edinburgh EH4 3EX
Telephone 031 315 2500
Contact: B C Tait[1], I Massie[2]
Investment Trusts
Dundee and London[1]
Dunedin Income Growth[1]
Dunedin Worldwide[1]
Edinburgh Investment[2]

For general enquiries use Freephone 0800 838993
Contact: Morag Kinnison/Robin Pollok

172

EDINBURGH FUND MANAGERS PLC

4 Melville Crescent, Edinburgh EH3 7JB
Telephone 031 226 4931

Contact: Marketing Dept.

Investment Trusts

American
British Investment
EFM Dragon
EFM Java
Malvern UK

ELECTRA KINGSWAY MANAGERS LTD

65 Kingsway, London WC2B 6QT
Telephone 071 831 6464

Contact: P J Dyke/J R Brown

Investment Trusts

Electra

FINSBURY ASSET MANAGEMENT LTD

Neptune House, Triton Court,
14 Finsbury Square, London EC2A 1BR
Telephone 071 256 8873

Contact: Ms Hilary Spivey

Investment Trusts

Lancashire & London
Scottish & Mercantile
Scottish Cities

FLEMING INVESTMENT TRUST MANAGEMENT LTD

25 Copthall Avenue, London EC2R 7DR
Telephone 071 920 0539

Contact: Bill Anderson

Investment Trusts

Fleming American
Fleming Claverhouse
Fleming Enterprise
Fleming European
Fleming Fledgeling
Fleming Far Eastern

Fleming Fledgeling
Fleming High Income
Fleming Int. High Income
Fleming Japanese
Fleming Mercantile
Fleming Overseas
Fleming Universal

FOREIGN & COLONIAL MANAGEMENT LTD

Exchange House, 8th Floor, Primrose Street,
London EC2A 2NY
Telephone 071 628 8000

Contact: Eleanor Brett

Investment Trusts

F&C Enterprise
F&C Eurotrust
F&C Germany
F&C Pacific

F&C Smaller Companies
Foreign and Colonial
Latin American

FRAMLINGTON INVESTMENT TRUST SERVICES

155 Bishopsgate, London EC2M 3XJ
Telephone 071 374 4100

Contact: Neil Killingback

Investment Trusts

New Throgmorton
Throgmorton Dual

Throgmorton Trust
Throgmorton USM

GT MANAGEMENT PLC

8 Devonshire Square (8th Floor), London EC2M 4YJ
Telephone 071 283 2575

**Contact: Paul Freeman/Barbara Edwards/
Andrew Watkiss**

Investment Trusts

Berry Starquest
GT Japan
USDC

GT VENTURE MANAGEMENT LTD

43-44 Albemarle Street, Mayfair, London W1X 3FE
Telephone 071 493 5685

Contact: Rhoddy Swire

Investment Trusts

GT Venture

GARTMORE INVESTMENT LIMITED

Gartmore House, 16 – 18 Monument Street,
London EC3R 3AJ
Telephone 071 623 1212

Contact: Philip Butt

Investment Trusts

English & Caledonian
English & Scottish
Gartmore American
Securities

Gartmore Emerging Pacific
Gartmore European
Gartmore Value Investments
London & Strathclyde

173

GARTMORE SCOTLAND LTD
Charles Oakley House, 125 West Regent Street,
Glasgow G2 2SG
Telephone 041 248 3972
Contact: Peter Kennedy
Investment Trusts
Scottish National

GLASGOW INVESTMENT MANAGERS LTD
29 St Vincent Place, Glasgow G1 2DR
Telephone 041 226 4585
Contact: Madeleine Stafford
Investment Trusts
Glasgow Income
Shires

GORDON HOUSE SECURITIES LTD
5 Half Moon Street, London W1Y 7RA
Telephone 071 409 3185
Contact: Jane Moir
Investment Trusts
The ECU Trust

JOHN GOVETT & CO LTD
Shackleton House, 4 Battle Bridge Lane,
London SE1 2HR
Telephone 071 378 7979
Contact: B R Jervis
Investment Trusts
Govett Atlantic
Govett Oriental
Govett Strategic

GRAHAMS RINTOUL & COMPANY LTD
Cologne House, 13 Haydon Street,
London EC3N 1DB
Telephone 071 488 1312
Contact: Peter Rintoul
Investment Trusts
Grahams Rintoul Investment Trust plc
North American Gas
Ralston

GROFUND INVESTMENT MANAGERS LTD
Young James House, 51 Belmont Road, Uxbridge,
Middlesex UB8 1RX
Telephone 0895 59783
Contact: John Rockett
Investment Trusts
First Ireland

GROSVENOR VENTURE MANAGERS LTD
Commerce House, 2 – 6 Bath Road, Slough SL1 3RZ
Telephone 0753 32623
Contact: Ray Thomas
Investment Trusts
Grosvenor Development Capital

GUINNESS MAHON INVESTMENT MANAGEMENT LTD
32 St Mary at Hill, London EC3P 3AJ
Telephone 071 623 9333
Contact: Miss A J Marsh
Investment Trusts
Temple Bar

HAMBRECHT & QUIST ASSET MANAGEMENT
c/o Ivory & Sime plc, One Charlotte Square, Edinburgh EH2 4DZ
Telephone 031 225 1357
Contact: Donald Robertson
Investment Trusts
London American Ventures Trust plc

174

HAMBROS BANK LIMITED
41 Tower Hill, London EC3N 4HA
Telephone 071 480 5000
Contact: F B Hyland
Investment Trusts
City of Oxford

HENDERSON ADMINISTRATION LIMITED
3 Finsbury Avenue, London EC2M 2PA
Telephone 071 638 5757
Contact: Geoffrey Dawson/Andrew Jardine

Investment Trusts
Electric & General   Lowland
English National   Strata
Greenfriar   Witan
Henderson Highland

IAN HENDERSON ASSOCS LTD
23 Cathedral Yard, Exeter EX1 1HB
Telephone 0392 412122
Contact: Ian Henderson
Investment Trusts
Dartmoor
Exmoor Dual
New Zealand

IVORY & SIME PLC
One Charlotte Square, Edinburgh EH2 4DZ
Telephone 031 225 1357
Contact: Investor Relations Dept

Investment Trusts
British Assets   Independent
Continental Assets   Investors Capital
First Charlotte Assets   Pacific Assets
I&S Optimum Income   Personal Assets
                           Selective Assets

JUPITER TARBUTT MERLIN LTD
11th Floor, Knightsbridge House,
197 Knightsbridge, London SW7 1RB
Telephone 071 581 8015
Contact: R H Ridout
Investment Trusts
Greyfriars
Merlin International Green
Primadona
River Plate & General Inv Trust plc

KLEINWORT BENSON DEVELOPMENT CAPITAL LTD
20 Fenchurch Street, London EC3P 3DB
Telephone 071 623 8000
Contact: Leonora Frost
Investment Trusts
Kleinwort Development

KLEINWORT BENSON INVESTMENT MANAGEMENT LTD
10 Fenchurch Street, London EC3M 3LB
Telephone 071 623 8000
Contact: Francis Ellison
Investment Trusts
Brunner   Kleinwort Overseas
Jos Holdings   Kleinwort Smaller
Kleinwort Charter   Companies
                           Merchants

LAURWOOD LIMITED
Lincoln House, 296/302 High Holborn, London WC1V 7JH
Telephone 071 404 8687
Contact: John C Walton
Investment Trusts
British Empire Securities and General Trust plc

THE LAW DEBENTURE CORPORATION PLC
Estates House, 66 Gresham Street,
London EC2V 7HX
Telephone 071 606 5451
Contact: Michael Caldicott

175

LLOYDS BANK FUND MANAGEMENT LTD
82 Queen Street, London EC4N 1SE
Telephone 071 600 4500
Contact: Mr W A Van Heesewijk
Investment Trusts
First Spanish
German
German Smaller Companies

LONDON & BISHOPSGATE INTERNATIONAL INVESTMENT MANAGEMENT PLC
12th Floor, 76 Shoe Lane, London EC4A 3JB
Telephone 071 583 1978
Contact: Larry Trachtenberg
Investment Trusts
First Tokyo Index

MARATHON ASSET MANAGEMENT
140a Gloucester Mansions,
Cambridge Circus, London WC2H 8HD
Telephone 071 497 2211
Contact: David Horne
Investment Trusts
Sphere

MARTIN CURRIE INVESTMENT MANAGEMENT LTD
29 Charlotte Square, Edinburgh EH2 4HA
Telephone 031 225 3811
Contact: J K R Falconer

Investment Trusts	
Martin Currie European	Scottish Eastern
Martin Currie Pacific	Securities Trust of
St Andrew	Scotland

MERCURY ASSET MANAGEMENT LTD
33 King William Street, London EC4R 9AS
Telephone 071 280 2800
Contact: Graham Wethered
Investment Trusts
Keystone

MEZZANINE CAPITAL & INCOME TRUST 2001 PLC
23 Cathedral Yard, Exeter EX1 1HB
Telephone 0392 412122
Contact: Clive Gaywood

MIM LTD
11 Devonshire Square, London EC2M 4YR
Telephone 071 626 3434
Contact: Gillian Wood

Investment Trusts	
City & Commercial	Drayton Far Eastern
Consolidated Venture	Leveraged Opportunity
Drayton Asia	Triplevest
Drayton Consolidated	
Drayton English & International	

MOORGATE INVESTMENT MANAGEMENT
49 Hay's Mews, London W1X 7RT
Telephone 071 409 3419
Contact: Anthony P Simonian
Investment Trusts
General Consolidated
Moorgate

MORGAN GRENFELL TRUST MANAGERS LTD
20 Finsbury Circus, London EC2M 1NB
Telephone 071 256 7500
Contact: Peggy Penhaligon
Investment Trusts
Anglo & Overseas
Overseas

MURRAY JOHNSTONE LTD
7 West Nile Street, Glasgow G1 2PX
Telephone 041 226 3131
Contact: Marjorie Calder
Investment Trusts
Murray Income
Murray International
Murray Smaller Markets
Murray Ventures

OLIM LTD
Pollen House, 10 – 12 Cork Street, London W1
Telephone 071 439 4400
Contact: Matthew Oakeshott
Investment Trusts
OLIM Convertible
Value & Income

PANTHER SECURITIES LTD
38 Mount Pleasant, London WC1X 0AP
Telephone 071 278 8011
Investment Trusts
Multitrust

PARIBAS ASSET MANAGEMENT (UK) LTD
68 Lombard Street, London EC2V 9LJ
Telephone 071 621 1161
Contact: Robin Kilborn
Investment Trusts
Paribas French

RIVER & MERCANTILE INVESTMENT MANAGEMENT LTD
7 Lincoln's Inn Fields, London WC2A 3BP
Telephone 071 405 7722
Contact: Vivien Gould
Investment Trusts
River & Mercantile
River & Mercantile American Capital & Income Growth
River & Mercantile Extra Income
River & Mercantile Geared Capital & Income 1999
River & Mercantile Smaller Companies

J ROTHSCHILD CAPITAL MANAGEMENT LTD
15 St James's Place, London SW1A 1NW
Telephone 071 493 8111
Contact: A Stafford-Deitsch
Investment Trusts
RIT Capital Partners

J ROTHSCHILD INVESTMENT MANAGEMENT LTD
15 St James's Place, London SW1A 1NW
Telephone 071 493 8111
Contact: Z H Schloss
Investment Trusts
Precious Metals Trust plc

N. M. ROTHSCHILD ASSET MANAGEMENT LTD
Five Arrows House, St Swithin's Lane,
London EC4N 8NR
Telephone 071 280 5000
Contact: N Paris
Investment Trusts
Equity Consort

SG INVESTMENT MANAGEMENT LIMITED
45 Bloomsbury Square, London WC1A 2RA
Telephone 071 242 5544
Contact: Richard Granville
Investment Trusts
Anglo Scandinavian

SCHRODER INVESTMENT MANAGEMENT LIMITED
36 Old Jewry, London EC2R 8BS
Telephone 071 382 6000

Contact: Alison Chong

Investment Trusts
Greece Fund
Korea-Europe Fund
Mediterranean Fund

SCOTTISH INVESTMENT TRUST PLC
6 Albyn Place, Edinburgh EH2 4NL
Telephone 031 225 7781

Contact: Alan P Jeffrey

STEWART IVORY & COMPANY LTD
45 Charlotte Square, Edinburgh EH2 4HW
Telephone 031 226 3271

Contact: James Ferguson

Investment Trusts
Scottish American

SUMIT EQUITY VENTURES LIMITED
Edmund House, 12 Newhall Street,
Birmingham B3 3ER
Telephone 021 200 2244

Contact: Nicholas Talbot Rice

Investment Trusts
SUMIT plc

3i PORTFOLIO MANAGEMENT LTD
91 Waterloo Road, London SE1 8XP
Telephone 071 928 3131

Contact: Robert McDougall

Investment Trusts
London Atlantic
North British Canadian

THORNTON INVESTMENT MANAGEMENT LIMITED
33 Cavendish Square, London W1M 7HF
Telephone 071 493 7262

Contact: Anthony Chancellor

Investment Trusts
Thornton Asian Emerging Markets
Thornton Pan European

TOUCHE, REMNANT & CO
Mermaid House, 2 Puddle Dock, London EC4V 3AT
Telephone 071 236 6565

Contact: Charles Hedgeland

Investment Trusts
Bankers'   TR Pacific
TR Far East Income   TR Property
TR City of London   TR Smaller Companies
TR European Growth   TR Technology
TR High Income

TRUST OF PROPERTY SHARES PLC
Fifth Floor, 77 South Audley Street, London W1Y 6EE
Telephone 071 486 4684

Contact: Mr Goodman

TYNDALL INVESTMENT MANAGEMENT LTD
25 Bucklersbury, London EC4N 8TH
Telephone 071 248 3399

Contact: Jayne Wigley

Investment Trusts
CST Emerging Asia   Pacific Horizon
European Project   Pacific Property
First Philippine
Korea Liberalisation

Also available from ROSTERS

The Right Job For You
Dr John Nicholson and Susan Clemie

Every week, newspapers around the U.K. carry ads for thousands of jobs, but it is often difficult to tell whether the job described is suitable for you. The authors of this book believe that, to find the right job, you must start by looking at yourself.

What makes you tick?' ('What do you enjoy doing?') ('What are you good at?') These are the questions to ask yourself — and these are the headings of the first three chapters in this book

To be happy and successful you need to choose the right type of job to suit your personality, natural talents and ambitions and this book will help you do just that. Aimed at those in a rut, or newcomers to the job market, here is a book that will help put sparkle back into your working life.

It includes:
- Your do-it-yourself personality profile
- How to identify your interests, skills and ambitions
- Matching your talents to various job requirements
- Winning strategies for job hunters

Training For Your Next Career
Margaret Korving

More and more people are choosing to change careers in mid-stream or perhaps, are forced to make a change due to redundancy. In this timely guide Margaret Korving shows you how to revolutionise your working life. She explains simply and clearly the choices open to you, the range of courses, variety of teaching methods and the cost of retraining.

It includes:
- Combining work with study
- On the job training and government schemes
- Studying from home
- Getting a degree
- Technician, craft, commercial professional courses

Your Green Career

Helen D'Arcy and Gillian Sharp

Can you stay green and still have a financially rewarding
job? The authors of this book show you how. It is packed
with practical advice on training, pay and job opportunities.
It includes interviews with people working in ''green'' jobs
across the country and shows you how to turn your talents
into a green career.

It includes:
● Healthy Alternatives
● Food For Thought
● Tilling The Soil
● All Creatures Great and Small
● The Great Outdoors
● National Heritage
● New Scientist
● Quality Control
● Building The Future

Fresh Start
Your Guide To Changing Careers By Men and Women Who Have Done It.
Dennis Barker

The symptoms are all too familiar. Lethargy, depression, inability to concentrate or cope with the daily grind at work. But, don't despair. It is possible to revitalise your life, reassess your priorities and rediscover that elusive job satisfaction. Dennis Barker, author and journalist, has talked to many people who have revolutionised their lives by the simple step of changing their careers. In this book they share their experiences and give positive guidance to others who may be contemplating a fresh start of their own.

It includes:
- Warning Signs
- Family Pressures Trap
- Paths to Giving
- Back to School
- Financial Step-down
- Resisting Ill Luck

All titles available at bookshops. If you have any problem getting the book you require, please contact the publishers Rosters Ltd at 23 Welbeck St, London W1M 7PG. Tel: 071-935 4550.